Living in 1984

America's Flirtation with Fascism

Gregg Ward Matson

Published by FastPencil

Published by FastPencil
307 Orchard City Drive
Suite 210
Campbell CA 95008 USA
info@fastpencil.com
(408) 540-7571
(408) 540-7572 (Fax)
http://www.fastpencil.com

Printed in the United States of America.

First Edition

To Sally C. Kuehne, who egged me on to write this book.

❧

Acknowledgments

A book that takes fifty years to write has many contributors. I will try to mention everyone who had a part in this one, knowing I will come up short. Deathless, eternally springing hope dares dream that this book will become a major work, and that everyone who feels he or she had even a small impact, will appreciate credit. Sneering, faithless "smart money" jokes that I am in the process of buying a garage full of books, and that nobody will care one way or another. Reality recognizes the results are out of my hands. For my part I know I worked long and hard, that completing this project was no small accomplishment. For this reason I want to thank everyone who took part in it.

Actually, everyone I have known has somehow, wittingly or not, contributed some life lesson that positively or negatively influenced this book. I cannot name them all. But I must start with Mom and Dad, who read in front of and to us kids and encouraged us to read. There was my eighth-grade English teacher, a Mr. Fox, who first mentioned 1984 in my hearing. When he said, apprehensively, "The really frightening thing about that book is—that it actually could happen," I was at once terrified and tempted. I had to read that book. It took a couple years to get the courage.

I have dedicated this book to my long-time friend Sally Kuehne, who vocally and often told me how much she liked my writing, and talked me into finally doing this project. There are the others my wife, Jolene, and I meet for coffee and fun: Alan Kuehne, Susan Burns, Wayne Bruns, Shelley Burns, Bill Dendle, Fritz Heilbron, Gwen Ayliffe, Katrina Ernst, Sean Hower. Sometimes we touched on serious subjects, which provoked my thoughts into words. Discussions of current affairs with close friends through the ages Steve and Angela Taylor, and Jenny and Hank Meyer, filled out my thoughts, and helped me to ascertain what I believe and to figure out how to say it.

And I was encouraged by the stalwart examples set by Glenn and Tracie Bailey, friends who routinely speak truth to power.

I am indebted to Steve Gates, an artist who does not know how good he is, for his arresting (pun intended) cover art. I have no way of expressing in mere words my gratitude to Lanny Hertzberg for taking the time to read the MS and write his concise Forward, describing in so few words exactly what I was hoping to do with this book.

My wife, Jolene, was with me all the way, patiently bearing my rants, ruthlessly and thoroughly editing my scribbles. She let me know what I needed to do in order to turn everything into something other people might be able to read. She encouraged me when I needed encouragement, and rendered honest and understandable criticism when I needed that. As faithfully as I could, I did as she suggested. Credit for this work's existence, not to mention readability, goes to her.

Surely I have missed some important contributions. As O'Brien says, in probably his only honest, humble, statement, "No book is produced individually, as you know." But we must move on. The year 1985 could be even worse.

Gregg Ward Matson, Elk Grove, California, February, 2014

Contents

Foreword

In this age of instant access to global information, one is often tempted to ignore the lessons of history so as to concentrate on the immediate. In fact it is almost required that we ignore the past because there is so much in the present to deal with. And in the present, exchanges of opinions have been reduced to 30 second sound bites and 140 character tweets. Gregg Matson has gone against the grain to try and reverse both of those trends. Using Orwell's "1984" as a base, Matson analyzes our present political society in depth. He not only compares our modern governmental system to Orwell's "Big Brother" in a point by point analysis, but he backs up his conclusions with a rigorous examination of the causes and events which led to our present situation.

While at times his description is so depressing that one feels like everything must indeed already be lost, Matson never lets the reader succumb to hopelessness. His book is instead a call to arms, an alarm bell whose ringing we ignore at our peril. He sees such efforts as the "Occupy Wallstreet" movement as indications that people can effect positive change. He sees hope for the majority of our population, because of our ability to communicate with each other in a relatively unfettered fashion. Matson has given us some tools to recognize the threat and it is up to us to collectively organize a response.

Alanson Hertzberg ~ Emeritus Professor of Anthropology and Computer Science, Cosumnes River College, Sacramento, California

Preface

WHY

In the summer of 1964, aged sixteen, I read *1984* and *Dracula*. By far the more frightening classic was Orwell's, because The Count was handicapped in his quest to turn people into mindless, undead slaves by the rules of the conflict between forces of good and evil. Big Brother, on the other hand, rigs the game wholly to his liking, uses old and new science to manipulate the worst in human nature, and never gets that hoped-for stake in the heart. Orwell's pessimistic ending, as opposed to Stoker's hopeful one, amply displays how radically our concepts of mankind's prospects changed in the fifty-two years between each novel's publication. The optimism of the late nineteenth century was gone by the middle of the twentieth. In the early part of the twenty-first, the question remains: Could the future really be "a boot stamping on a human face—forever"?

In 1964, Oceania was at war with Eastasia (China) and was allied with Eurasia (Russia). This had always been the perceived reality. Forgotten was the time, only a few years earlier, when Oceania had always been at war with Eastasia and Eurasia. By the early seventies, Oceania would be always at war with Eurasia, and allied with Eastasia. So it would go. There are some variations on Orwell's three predicted super-states, in the early twenty-first century. Eurasia has, for practical purposes, divided into two super-states, one with a capital at Moscow, the other with capitals in Paris and Berlin. India, which Orwell predicted would be a colony, is becoming a major super-state. Eastasia is in two parts: China, and a looser alliance led by Japan, including South Korea, Taiwan, and eventually, Vietnam. Latin America appears to be forming a super-state apart from Oceania. Then there is the nebulous non-state of radical Islam; though not a country, it is still an enemy. Any one, or combination, of these super-states could be the next forever enemy. The media will keep us informed about whom we hate.

Modern dictators need permanent warfare. Only the ongoing fear of foreign enemies can induce people to give up their freedom. Only war can excuse widespread privation and deterioration of infrastructure. The goal of rulers is to promise inevitable victory while keeping war—any war—going. After all, in times of peace, citizens begin to demand a share in its rewards. This is a major premise of *1984*, and it holds true. Modern dictators also need a big lie, and a sophisticated delivery system for it. Obviously, the West has perfected advertising to a point where virtually anything and everything can be sold to a gullible public. Those who wax wealthy on this system have managed to take control of our economics and politics, and they are determined to maintain their control. With the Citizens' United decision the Supreme Court gave corporate interests an ultimate weapon. If We the People fail to reverse that decision with a Constitutional Amendment denying corporate personhood, America will have arrived at fascism.

What is truly frightening about "Citizens' United" is the fact that the American people have brought this grim circumstance upon themselves, by electing over the last thirty plus years, presidents who have appointed justices who believe corporations are human. All U.S. presidents have been pro-business. Some of them have actually sought to curb corporate control over everybody else, but no true anti-corporate candidates have ever come even remotely close to being elected. In recent times, however, the corporate machine has grown increasingly skillful at electing presidents who represent corporate interests and no other. Cheerleaders for the corporate side work diligently to label any president who tries to also serve the people as "socialist." A demonstrated intolerance for opposition has emerged among the right wing, and it is growing more rigid in its refusal to compromise.

Modern dictators need a large and vocal group of citizens (not necessarily a majority) who believe the Big Lie to where they will vote against their own self-interests. The ranks of these "True Believers" swell in times of rapid social and economic change, times of information overload.

Obviously, the twentieth century was fertile ground, and the twenty- first promises to be more fertile still. The unknown is whether the tiny minority comprising the corporate class can control the true believers whom they hope to manipulate in order to maintain power. So far they have been successful, but history shows different results over the long run, results that are disastrous for everyone.

The antidote to corporate power lies in "We the People." We must work constantly and together to curb and reverse the takeover of our democracy by corporate power. It will not do for us to lock the doors, stockpile food and guns, and hide. "Eternal vigilance is the price of liberty." We need to act on what we see.

Introduction

This book is arranged into four sections: "War is Peace," "Ignorance is Strength," "Freedom is Slavery," and "The Schoolyard Bully." The first three are taken from the main slogans of the Ingsoc Party, and the chapters within are my observations measuring the extent which our current reality coincides with the Party's stated goals in Orwell's scenario. Since the slogans are interdependent, the discussions of course must overlap. The fourth section explores the common mentality of autocratic rulers, that we might get a glimpse of their level of maturity and emotional stability. A glossary of terms Orwell originated in *1984* is set at the end of this book.

The hope is that we can make decisions on whether we want such people to run our lives. Having made our decisions, we can begin dialogue on what actions to take. The observations made in this book are not meant to be exclusive.

My intent is to coax people into committing "thoughtcrime."

A Brief Summary of 1984

(NOT a substitute for reading or re-reading the classic novel.)

Winston Smith, a minor functionary of the English Socialist (Ingsoc) Party living in London, has been feeling disloyal to the dictatorship of Big Brother lately. He intends to commit treason, or in Ingsoc terms, "thoughtcrime", by starting a diary. He knows the act of writing in a diary is treason, but so is thinking about it. And he knows he will ultimately get caught, because: "Big Brother is Watching You." And everyone else.

Big Brother, hallowed leader of the Party and the nation (Oceania) knows all, though whether he really exists is never shown. Still, everyone knows he is watching. The year is 1984, though no one ever keeps track of years anymore. There is only now, and the moment is forever, before and after. The moment's truth is whatever the party line says it is. The party line could change instantly, and eventually will, and the changes will be the truth, now, and always. To recall that the party line was different in the past is another treasonous form of thoughtcrime.

Winston begins a romance with Julia, a young Party member. Their mutual attraction is also against Party rules, because people are expected to be passionate only toward the Party and Big Brother.

Winston's boss, a Party leader named O'Brien, befriends Winston and Julia, and shows sympathy for their feelings and their rebelliousness. He introduces them to a revolutionary underground organization called The Brotherhood, and begins to school them in the secret methods of resistance. Once they become totally confident, O'Brien has them arrested. Winston undergoes a long period of rehabilitation through mental and physical torture, under O'Brien's supervision. Winston and Julia betray each other, confess to heinous crimes against the state, and become mindlessly loyal, incapable of resistance by deed, word, or even thought.

George Orwell's frightening look at life in a modern dictatorship is a warning. His adept transplanting of life in Nazi Germany or Soviet Russia onto the democratic world leaves us with no illusions that we are immune. Continuous warfare uses up surplus production and keeps the population afraid, vulnerable to authoritarian rule. People get used to steady propaganda and government spying. Opportunists seize control; tyranny becomes commonplace and entrenched. Orwell observed that the long privations of WWII and the immediate postwar period could last forever. He told the story intending to scare us into doing what we need to do to avoid its coming true.

At an Occupy demonstration, someone carried a sign reading: "1984 WAS NOT MEANT TO BE AN INSTRUCTION MANUAL." Some protest signs tell a simple, genuine truth. This one is in my opinion the most accurate description of what is going on in America in the beginning of the Third Millennium. Many of us in the American Empire—Oceania—know something is amiss about our standings as individuals, our relation to our government, our access to facts. Like Winston Smith, remembering a news clipping he saw once that proved Big Brother told lies, we are vaguely aware that we are being led in a direction that we would rather not follow. And we sense that we are powerless to prevent it. We sense, if we dare to admit it, that we have lost our democracy.

We look at the history of Soviet Russia and Nazi Germany (which Orwell skillfully planted on our own political scene) and shake our heads. We can see myriad superficial dissimilarities between Orwell's horror story and our lives today. The year 1984 came and went, and we still have our democratic institutions, private property, and private lives. Though Big Brother does watch us, we can criticize our leaders without fear of being vaporized. So maybe we have nothing to worry about. Too much coffee, too much stimulation from television shows that fail to entertain. If we exercise more, eat healthier, work harder—we are sure to get over our uneasiness.

Or will we? When we look back at the year 1984, we were at war with Russia, and we had always been, and always would be. Here in the second decade of the Twenty-first Century we are at war with militant fanatical Islamic jihad, and this has gone on, and will go on, seemingly forever…until of course the final victory. And until that victory, we are bound to accept whatever edicts our leadership sends down to us. Our communications are monitored. Vague discomforts are not readily dismissed. Yes, the autocratic controls over individuals are much more subtle than in Orwell's classic, but the desire of our elites for more power over everyone else seems to be as obsessive as ever. Economic destruction of the middle class is obvious and ongoing, and this destruction, while causing untold misery, also renders more power to the upper class.

Americans are not ready to submit to the brutal totalitarian tactics of the Nazis, the Bolsheviks, or the Ingsoc Party. Those who seek absolute power in our modern society are aware of this, and they will use less force if it will obtain their objectives. But in autumn 2013, the United

States government was shut down by a fanatical minority of congressmen, financed by a few incredibly wealthy individuals, promoted by a slick television, radio, and internet propaganda network. Without a functioning government, the only organizations capable of operating a complex modern society are corporations. Yet, the nation still maintains foreign wars and internal and external spying networks. This situation defines fascism. The protest sign has become prophecy.

OBSERVATIONS ON FASCISM

DEFINITIONS OF FASCISM:

fascism n 1.) a governmental system with strong centralized power, permitting no opposition or criticism, controlling all affairs of the nation (industrial, commercial, etc.) emphasizing an aggressive nationalism and (often) anti-communist. *American College Dictionary*

fascism—noun—an authoritarian and nationalistic right-wing system of government and social organization, (in general use) extreme right-wing, authoritarian, or intolerant views or practice. *Oxford Dictionary Online*

Fascism:

1. Often capitalized, a political philosophy, movement or regime (as that of the Fascisti) that exalts a nation and often race above the individual and that stands for a centralized autocratic government headed by a dictatorial leader, severe economic and social regimentation, and forcible suppression of opposition.
2. a tendency toward or actual exercise of strong autocratic or dictatorial control. *Webster Online*

fascism…n. 1. A philosophy or system of government that advocates or exercises a dictatorship of the extreme right, typically through the merging of state and business leadership, together with an ideology of belligerent nationalism. *American Heritage Dictionary*

"Fascism should be called corporatism, as it is the merging of government and corporate power." - Benito Mussolini

Whether Mussolini or his ghostwriter, Gentile, truly wrote the definition of fascism, it is clear that Il Duce understood and approved. Much of

Orwell's descriptions of "English Socialism" are based on the immense impoverishment and insane brutality of Stalinism, but all totalitarian dictatorships fit here, with only small details separating them. It requires no stretch of the imagination to see the National Socialism (Nazi) and English Socialism (Ingsoc) connection. Fascists may cheer free enterprise just as Bolsheviks cheer the working class, but reality shows neither to be important to modern totalitarians of any professed philosophy. Their contempt for the people they claim to represent is the outstanding feature. In all cases, State power controls everything, and people who work for a living are viewed as problems to control.

Whatever the system's name, if most or all of the definitions of fascism apply, then a nation is under a fascist dictatorship. Orwell's terrifying descriptions of total control and ruthless torture have millions of true examples. To anyone unfortunate enough to become mired in a dictatorship's penal system, the stated mission of the ruling clique is of no import. As Winston Smith found out, all a victim of the Thought Police wants is to stop the pain.

The Bolsheviks banished private property, but shrewd insiders were able to game the system and amass large fortunes, in reality if not in title. All things considered, Stalin at his death was the sole owner of nine million square miles under his rule. Fascists and Nazis protected private property, but only at the very highest level. With Big Business holding supreme economic power, fascist dictators are naturally anti-communist. It goes without saying, so is the United States. But now that communism has lost the Cold War, have we reached that future which, as Ronald Reagan gloated, "belongs to the free?" How free are we, here in the nation that protected freedom for so long?

Answering these questions in this book is not as important as encouraging others to ask these questions. We Baby Boomers had fathers who fought in WWII, to protect our freedom and free others who had been oppressed. Roosevelt and Churchill met on January 6, 1941, to lay out the "Four Freedoms": Freedom of speech and religion, freedom from want and fear. These were the goals of Oceania in WWII—far different from O'Brien's "God is Power." However, Stalin also won WWII (Russia, obviously, did not) and the resources of the Free World were re-focused to ward off a communist takeover: war with Eurasia.

Anti-communism does not automatically mean democracy. Being against an anti-communist war does not imply communist sympathies. The measure of our freedom lies in how well we are able to accept differences of opinion, and how well we reach compromise that we can work with. Of course compromise satisfies no one. But no one is satisfied with absolute power either. We still have the trappings of republican government, but we have also lived in a garrison state since WWII. And with that mentality we have allowed a small corporate minority to gain immense economic power over us, resulting in growing income inequality and the social subservience that inequality entails. Our democratic institutions are in many ways cosmetic only. Polls in every part of the country show that large majorities support public schools, parks, libraries, health services, and a functioning infrastructure. Still many of our leaders dismiss these as frivolous or prohibitively expensive. At the same time military budgets are increased. Much of the media have abandoned their traditional adversarial roles, and now find ways to back up the corporate line.

Perhaps the greatest impediment to progress in the latter twentieth and early twenty-first centuries is that Stalin and Mao called themselves socialists. Their brutal pursuit of absolute power in the name of "the people" has allowed spokespeople for corporate interests to cry the foul of "socialism" to any proposal to increase taxes on the wealthy, or to employ people on public works projects. Even programs with solid citizen support, such as Social Security and Medicare, are labeled socialistic, and their supporters are forced to defend them in debate. Even though it is well known that no one has gone to the Gulag due to Social Security, the rightwing continues to shout about the menace. Social democrats like Orwell and Upton Sinclair were among the most strident denouncers of the Bolsheviks, but right-wingers in the mass media have been relentless about lumping social democrats with the fascists who call themselves socialists. It serves the corporate elites in Oceania to boast about our freedom while pointing fingers at the autocratic darkness in socialist Eurasia and Eastasia.

Orwell pointed out that the differences in actual life in all three super-states were small. The "Four Freedoms" can serve as indicators for the health of our cherished democracy. We can also examine the Declaration of Independence to ascertain how well we are securing those "inalienable rights…Life, Liberty, and the Pursuit of Happiness." Upon examination, we can then decide what to do. We must act, and together, in order to preserve and enhance our freedom. Orwell was issuing a warning, not making a prediction. The price of liberty has always been eternal vigilance, and complacency squanders our liberty. If we ever find ourselves "looking, with knowledge, at a member of the Thought Police," it will be too late.

Part 1 - War is Peace

1

Speculations on Reality

"Throughout recorded time, and probably since the end of the Neolithic Age, there have been three kinds of people, the High, the Middle, and the Low ....

The aims of these three groups are entirely irreconcilable. The aim of the High is to remain where they are. The aim of the Middle is to change places with the High. The aim of the Low, when thy have an aim—for it is an abiding characteristic of the Low that they are too much crushed by drudgery to be more than intermittently conscious of any thing outside their daily lives—is to abolish all distinctions and create a society in which all men shall be equal." - 1984

It's only class warfare when we fight back.

With the proles reduced to drudgery, the High class only needs to subjugate the Middle. This process comprises the plot of 1984, and this book will explore the extent to which it is happening in 2014. If class warfare has been constant reality since the start of complex agricultural society, it would stand to reason that one of the most effective weapons of the High to stay that way would be to convince the two classes below them that there is no such thing as class warfare. Spokespersons for the elites are quick to respond to proposals to make it easier for those who work for a living to get a living, with warnings about "class warfare," the unstated point being that in the United States we have no classes, that all of us have the same chances to improve our lot. Corollary to this Big Lie is that poor people are poor because they are lazy, stupid, or burdened with handicaps that prevent their working hard to better their status. At any rate, the wealthy believe they have taken advantage of their good fortune to be born in this class-free land of opportunity, so they should therefore be left to enjoy the fruits of their labour undisturbed by envious underlings.

Plainly, the wealthy in our society, as in any other, like where they are, and strive to stay there. They pay handsomely those who can make convincing arguments that they deserve their privileges. As plain is the fact that the suffering in the current Great Recession is borne solely by the Middle and Lower classes. Those who must work for a living, be that living comfortable or barely enough to get by, are being ruthlessly squeezed by the tight economy. And whether the Great Recession is a direct result of class warfare waged by the elites, it is plain that the middle class has been routed to the point where it poses no threat to the power of the elites. And it is the wealthy, with their servants in the media, who oppose any attempts to use government to restore some economic balance, or even a little security, to the general economy.

Thirty years after the year 1984, the middle class is reduced to virtual wage slavery (when there are jobs), working longer and harder than ever, for less pay and reduced, even disappearing benefits. Whether individuals within the middle class actually want to replace or join the upper class, current conditions have rendered them incapable of doing so. The general standard of living has been drastically reduced. The social contract and the infrastructure we all depend on are crumbling. Yet our military still devours immense portions of our material productivity, and we are not even granted an honest debate on whether the consumption is needed. We are told we are at war, or soon will be, that to question military readiness only plays into the hands of the enemy. War keeps the powerful in power.

Corporate boardrooms convey the same message as the Inner Ingsoc Party: "Thou art." In the corporate world absolute obedience and loyalty—to the firm instead of the party—hold the key to individual success. Every corporation has a party line, though company men and women refrain from using that term. Directives from on high carry the weight of divine edicts, and all who hear them are expected to concur in mind, heart, and soul. Never mind if today's directive is the opposite of yesterday's. That fact goes down the memory hole, and fellow climbers on the corporate ladder constantly watch one another for any sign of disagreement or discontent. The powers that be have no use for critical thinking or well-meaning questions. Though the capitalist creed worships "rugged individualism" as a concept, just as the Soviet Empire praised "the people," the rulers actually tolerate only absolute loyalty. They need no Ministry of Love to enforce it. The deteriorating economy is more effective and far cheaper.

There is always the possibility that the middle class and the working poor, who have been squeezed into identical social and economic straights, could recognize their common situation and band together to challenge corporate power. The Occupy movements of 2011 had a real chance to do just this, but the power structure waited them out. The potential is still there, though the masses remain satisfied with the huge smorgasboard of bread and circuses the electronic world provides (with the bonus that the plebes actually pay for their entertainment). Furthermore, the Ministry of Truth in our world has been handed a monstrous gift courtesy of the Supreme Court, in the Citizens' United decision.

While the ruling elites currently need no brutal police state methods to stay in power, they have at hand all the tools Big Brother had, only far more sophisticated. More fearsome is that millions of American citizens feel no compunction toward using the police state, as long as it is used on "those people." Politicians who promote torture are quite successful in elections, and even those who would do away with torture must defend themselves against charges of "anti-Americanism." Partisans of torture know what they never say: torture works—not to reveal truth, but to obtain confessions to any and all accusations. Almost everybody who undergoes torture will ultimately admit guilt, a happy fact for the torturers, since they consistently prove they are never wrong.

Though people who are vaporized and tortured come out of the system broken if they come out at all, probably no ruling elite can retain absolute power forever. Human nature is resilient and unpredictable. We have witnessed the downfall of the supposedly invincible Soviet Union. Mao's fanatical communism has given way to "practical men of action" wearing suits.

Neither Eurasia (Russia) nor Eastasia (China) has become democratic, by any means. Still, Orwell died before the sequel, in which about 1990, O'Brien and Big Brother himself were vaporized. But the failure of Orwell's nightmare scenario to come true literally does not mean we have nothing to worry about. The media apparatus serving the elites grows more sophisticated. Class warfare is never mentioned unless the lower classes make serious efforts to change things for their benefit. Meanwhile warfare goes on, wasting production that could make life easier for everyone. And the holy cause behind any particular police state is meaningless to anyone who is ensnared in the system. Whether a dictatorship is communist, fascist, tinhorn general or divine right monarch—or beacon of democracy—life in political prison is pretty much the same.

2

The Price of Freedom

"Hard climb ahead to reverse losses… Middle-Class recovery will take years, PEW report says." - *Sacramento Bee, 8/23/2012*

"Proles and animals are free." - *1984*

The Populists of the late nineteenth century and the Progressives of the early twentieth offered plausible alternatives to robber baron capitalism. So effective were they that both capitalist parties pre-empted their major programs, in order to prevent these movements from taking power. And there were always the Socialists, Bolsheviks, and Wobblies, who really stirred up the workers' anger. While the State incarcerated and brutalized them, radicals still had great appeal. The ruling classes, not only in the United States but throughout the industrialized world, had to make at least some attempts to heed the demands of the proletariat. The workers and rulers eventually compromised: the capitalists could go on exploiting workers, while the workers got some say in how to make the exploitation more tolerable.

World War I, when unfettered capitalism reached its catastrophic logical conclusion, cemented the partnership. The rulers of all nations needed their proletarians to kill the proles who served their enemies. Nationalism trumped worker solidarity, and poor men worldwide died by the millions. The poor were rewarded in some nations with democratic reforms, in others with some form of fascism. The great hope everywhere was for no more war. Even the robber barons had been chastened by the carnage, the price of unbridled greed.

The war had illuminated the problem created by industrialization: that production outstripped the ability of workers to buy what they had made.   Without extensive re-distribution of wealth, and reduction of demands on individual labour, the world would be glutted with products no one could buy. Rather than deal with this new reality thoughtfully, the world's elites chose to intensify the brutality of already fierce competition by making war to kill off their excess workers and destroy excess production. The elites did not consciously conspire in this effort, anymore than coyotes conspire to kill sheep. But war was more suited to the nature of the rulers than sharing, which would have ended their reign.

The goal in WWI was for one set of elites to dominate the others. But mass production had also enabled mass destruction, and the horrors of war were indelibly tattooed on human conscience. In the ensuing case of global shell shock, some rulers lost their countries. Those who remained had lost their confidence.

The scarcely recovered status quo was shaken again by the Great Depression. A scant decade after the war to end all wars, over-production happened again. But this time war was not the first option. Economic stimulus on a Keynesian model was tried in much of the industrialized world. The wealthy resisted, but on a smaller scale than they had before, on the principle of rugged individualism. Privation and poverty on a large scale were preferable, in their viewpoint, to government handouts and a socialist nanny state. Despite some one-sided elections against their positions, the elites were able to slow down the New Deal, to the point where the country was still in a mild depression when WWII kick-started the economy once more.

Right wingers like to gloat that it was WWII, not the New Deal, that brought us back to full employment and prosperity. They employ double-think here, by which they can ignore the fact that WWII was a public works project on an enormous scale, employing sixteen million Americans directly, and everyone else in war production. The nation's, indeed the world's, citizenry was once again fully utilized to produce things to be destroyed.

Orwell observes in *1984* that war as public works is universally acceptable, in contrast with projects to employ people to build lasting things for the peaceful public welfare. Perhaps the urgency of war sets off predictable human impulses, the belief that anything and everything must be done to achieve victory. Perhaps war simply appeals to the robber baron mentality. At any rate, the champions of rugged individualism were not then, and are not now, opposed to that ultimate destroyer of all individualism, war.

After WWII a rough partnership was set in place between the workers and owners, to the overall benefit of society. Rich and poor alike prospered. People from the middle and lower classes could (and some did) get rich. A social safety net made survival possible for many who were left behind in those troublesome times when supply overwhelmed demand. Roads, dams, schools, parks (among others) employed people who bought things, stimulating the private sector. And the good old arms race was always around, using up surplus production worldwide.

But even though the rich were richer, and there were more rich people than ever, the fact of average working folks getting a good living seemed to bother some rich people. As the philosophers have said for thousands of years, wealth does not bring fulfillment, joy, or self-esteem. Rather than seek other avenues toward happiness, some rich people have simply sought more riches at the expense of those who are not rich. Since greed, like all other addictions, has no limits, we should not be shocked to see that its unimpeded practice can have anti-social results. To the charge of "anti-social", Margaret Thatcher denies any such possibility by claiming "There is no society." Thatcher and Ronald Reagan together led Oceania's transformation from moderate social democracy back to untamed plutocracy.

With the claim that our complex modern society was in reality an illusion, went the doublethink myth that we really do have a society, but it is classless, so the capitalist world has actually achieved the delusional goal of Marxism. As the myth goes: surely, we have classes. After all a socialite is not going to freely associate with a vagrant. But since the vagrant could, if he applied himself, get rich, we indeed have a classless society. And since we do have a society without class lines, it stands to reason that the wealthy have earned their wealth, therefore no one has a right to take any of that wealth to help anyone else. The height of Western civilization came at the end of the nineteenth century when ruthless competition between determined rugged individuals allowed the accumulation of great wealth, which left most others in abject poverty—then were men "truly free." Reagan, Thatcher, and many other high priests of wealthy privilege, made their point over and over, until ultimately, some in the lesser classes believed it.

The prophets of greed were able to gain dominance thanks to several shocking events of the seventies: Watergate, the energy shortage, the Iranian hostage crisis, stagflation of the economy. But the Vietnam War was what stopped the New Deal cold. That conflict , by using up virtually all the nation's surplus production, graphically demonstrated Orwell's prediction of waging limited warfare to keep the citizens poor. With resources suddenly in short supply, it was possible to stop the blending of classes, so the elites could stay where they were.

But the limited war in Vietnam was not limited enough. Too much blood was shed, enough of it American to revive memories of the horrors of war. Protest movements had flourished, and a mostly peaceful revolution had begun. At the point where the elites had gained economic control, they were faced with the possibility of losing social and political control. So while Reagan called the Vietnam War a "noble cause", and an overall complaisant media let it go, the ruling elites made a point of continuing the permanent war by picking weak enemies, thus greatly reducing American casualties and keeping the conflicts short and glorious. The eighties saw enormous consolidation of economic, political, and social processes in the hands of the wealthy.

The elites skillfully disarmed the anti-war and civil rights movements, before they could work into the mainstream of the political system, before they could become modern Progressives or Populists. By repeating the "noble cause" big lie, their spokespeople eliminated much of the terrible memory of the Vietnam War. New assaults in the "War on Drugs" further stigmatized anyone who had been associated with the anti-war movement. Concerning civil rights, Reagan's revival of states' rights served to warn many whites in the working class that resources were thin, and sharing with "those people" would hamper their own living standards. Besides, "those people" could do better if they would work. Doublethink got people who were benefiting from government social spending to believe that they had acquired and achieved solely by their own gumption. The never-ending "two-minute hates" (they actually lasted longer) of whatever enemy we had at the moment kept us from paying close attention to what was actually going on: the elites had seized power, and were in the serious process of consolidating it. 1984 happened more or less right on schedule.

3

The Manly Art of War

"I fought in Iraq to preserve your freedoms, you liberal pussy." (seen on a bumper sticker)

"A peace that was truly permanent would be the same as permanent war. This—although the vast majority of party members understand it only in a shallower sense—is the inner meaning of the Party slogan: WAR IS PEACE." - *1984*

The first quote, a fine example of doublethink, tersely though unintentionally makes the case that war dumbs down debate. Our *Constitution* allows someone to paste such sentiments on his bumper. These sentiments tell the world that meaningful dialogue with the bumper's owner is impossible...just in case the world wanted to know. It could be construed as a desperate cry for help, delivered in a way that virtually no such help will be forthcoming. It also shields the elites who sent him to war from criticism, and allows them to find new wars to wage, to the point where war never stops, and so becomes peace. A bumper sticker, representing the vehicle owner's rights, recognizes that even people who disagree with him have rights, yet in its hostile intolerant nature assures all concerned that no rights will actually be exercised. Like it or not, this is an admirable piece of propaganda.

The Iraq War was not in reality fought for freedom. A rogue's gallery of neocon advisors, such as Wolfowitz, Perle, Feith, and Rumsfeld, allied with an equally loathsome coterie of fortune hunters from the military-industrial complex led by Richard Cheney, prevailed upon a phenomenally lazy and uninformed president to invade. Americans' liberties were not at stake in Iraq. If Saddam Hussein's ouster did in fact enhance the liberties of the people of Iraq, the measure of increased freedom must be stacked against the loss of life, limb, and societal stability that the U.S. invasion wrought. Civil liberties were curtailed in the United States. Protests with turnouts in record numbers failed to stop the rush to war. A system has been arisen which marginalizes and ignores grassroots opposition to the policies serving the elites. It is as effective as, and far cheaper than, censorship, persecution, and imprisonment. For all their bravery, dedication, and efficiency, American troops did not kill and die for anyone's rights.

When a nation is at war it becomes harder for citizens to take action against any governmental action, even those that have nothing to do with the prosecution of the war. The Founding Fathers knew this, which was why they tried to make it difficult for the country to go to war. Ideally, if the Congress, being closer to the people than any other branch of government, cannot agree on warfare, then the nation stays out of war. Presidents have historically been resourceful about finding ways around this troublesome impediment to executive power, but early in our history chief executives have had to tread lightly: small wars, quickly ended, or else Congress got involved. The Indian wars were nearly always out of sight and mind to most Americans. But since WWII, the American Empire needed, and found, ways to circumvent the intentionally slow constitutional process. Sometimes a president will ask permission—in reality asking Congress to abdicate its constitutional duty—but he always expects to get that permission.   Sometimes the president will actually disobey laws against going to war, as happened with Nicaragua in the eighties. The Reagan administration was caught giving military aid to the Nicaraguan contras, although Congress had prohibited U.S. involvement in Nicaragua's internal affairs. Adding insult to injury, the administration had been financing the Contra War by selling arms to Iran, which had also been forbidden by Congress. Hearings followed, which embarrassed Reagan slightly, but most of the blame fell on underlings, and some commentators even blamed congressmen for sabotaging the war effort. Presidential privilege prevailed in matters of war, and the whole affair was forgotten when the next two-minutes hate started.

Since the *Constitution* is specific about who has the authority to engage the nation in warfare, we can conclude that the Law of the Land has been, in this case, cruelly mauled. And since wars are waged and forgotten so routinely, we can conclude that War now is Peace. Doublethink is triumphant. A veteran can put up an offensive bumper sticker like the one at the head of this chapter, with complete immunity from argument within "polite" society. In truth he risked life, limb, and sanity in a useless venture based on false pretenses, which had no impact on national security. He is understandably angry, but his anger is directed at those who were on his side— a situation that greatly benefits the elites who sent him to bleed in that far—off land. Contrary to his belief, he did not fight for our freedom. In reality, his sacrifices restricted our freedom. He was conned, as were the rest of us, even those of us who were aware of the scam from the outset. We lost our freedom to oppose war, which indicates the next one is about to start.

War is Peace.

4

The Few, The Brave

"But in a physical sense, war involves very small numbers of people, mostly highly trained specialists, and causes comparatively few casualties. The fighting, when there is any, takes place on the vague frontiers whose whereabouts the average man can only guess at." - *1984*

No one doubts that the angry veteran of the previous chapter fought bravely, performed his duties with a high level of skill, is dedicated and patriotic. These accolades, and more, are genuinely deserved by America's modern professional military personnel. When ordered to attack, conquer, and occupy a hostile foreign country, they did their job well. If ordered to protect our freedoms they would do so, and our freedoms would be preserved. In all our history there is no finer example of military prowess than exists in the marrow of America's modern professional military. The old perceptions of a citizen military, made somewhat clownish in *The Caine Mutiny*, *Slaughterhouse-Five* or *Catch-22* (among many fine books) are no longer applicable. Nor are the grim, resentful accounts that caused the military establishment to come unglued in Vietnam. The American soldiery of the twenty-first century is as worthy as a human establishment can get.

Unfortunately, as they are part of the human race, American military people have human shortcomings, foremost in this case being that they can be killed or wounded, or sent home with mental demons that require a lifetime of focused effort to overcome. Because of these human frailties, it is officially convenient to ignore the plight of veterans, to ignore even their commendable actions, once the reality of war sets in. And after ten years in Iraq and twelve in Afghanistan, the reality is obvious and everywhere. Some veterans are forced to depend on charity for treatment of their physical and mental injuries. At the same time, some members of Congress are determined to spend hundreds of millions of dollars to build tanks that the Army does not want. Remembrances of the cheers and parades with which the troops were sent to war are down the memory hole. Proposals for war against Syria are met with universal disapproval, which bodes well for potential peace.

Remembering the casualties reminds us that war has far outlived any usefulness it might once have had. When citizens start to relate to the dead, the maimed, and their families, war becomes part of the national consciousness…in short, war is no longer peace. War, once it is known for what it really is, had better have an important goal, and an end, lest people begin asking serious questions. And once they start asking questions, they will continue asking questions to which the rulers have few, if any, plausible answers.

In a democracy, which we still have in form, society would look after the needs of bereaved relatives and friends, the ones who must take back the ruined refuse of war. The survivors would be helped—not simply cheered once, then forgotten. The true cost of war would be borne by all. An aware population would challenge the authorities' next proposal for war. People are aware now, which is why the desire to bomb Syria gets no traction outside the Washington establishment. Seriously questioning war was virtually useless from the end of Vietnam to Iraq, as anyone who tried to question war fever during that period learned quickly. Our country's relentless pursuit of undeclared war reveals how extensively our democracy has been eroded, how used to war we have become. But with the horrible reality of our two most recent wars so much in evidence, we are momentarily aware of the cost—in lives lost and ruined, fortune squandered, and misery spread around. From the tragedy comes an opportunity to reclaim our democracy for people. The mass media that the elites use so adroitly to manipulate public opinion can be used to inform us all of the truth.

War is not peace unless it happens to somebody else. Americans have awakened to the fact that we are in our wars together. At this time, we know the difference between war and peace. Allowed to make a choice, people will almost always choose peace. They will exercise their rights, which will cause the entire power structure to unravel. It is essential for any group of elites wanting to remain elite to keep the public desperately unaware. Ongoing small war accomplishes this goal. Wars keep people angry and mistrustful of one another, and they use up surplus production so the masses remain, if not poor, at least financially insecure. Iraq and Afghanistan got too big. They raised the consciousness of citizens, which allowed the election of at least some politicians whose allegiance to the military-industrial complex could not be taken for granted. More importantly, citizens are informing politicians in no uncertain terms that we are not ready for more war. In 2014, war is not peace, and we all know it. This is a moment of rare opportunity to stop living in 1984.

5

Backdrop to 1984

"Theoreticians of the Kremlin hardly waited for the guns of the Second World War to cool before they picked the democratic West, and particularly America, as the chosen enemy. It is doubtful whether any gesture of goodwill or any concession on our side will reduce the volume of venom and vilification against us emanating from the Kremlin." - Eric Hoffer, *The True Believer*

We can tell now that at least some of the big thinkers in the Pentagon felt the same way toward Russia at the end of WWII. The shift in thinking came about smoothly: we were at war with Eurasia, and we had always been at war with Eurasia. Why else would allied agents have swept through Germany with the troops, picking up scientists, fixing them with credentials proving they never really were Nazis, that they only followed orders? An interesting aside, exemplifying doublethink, is that the obedience excuse, which was declared in the Nuremberg trials to be invalid for people like Ribbentrop, worked without a glitch for Von Braun and others whose knowledge could be put to use in the war that had already started, that had always been going on. After all, capitalism (free enterprise and rugged individualism) had been at war with Bolshevism (collectivism, dictatorship) at least since 1848. So we could forget the recent alliance we had forged with Stalin. At any rate, the holocaust was a crime against humanity gross enough to get people hanged, while sending missiles to blow up cities and kill women, children, and civilians was a much-needed skill. And shrewdly, both emerging super-states sent agents to recruit men who had that skill, probably even before American and Russian soldiers were photographed toasting one another as they met on the field of victory.

Another craft much sought by both sides in the new forever war was the science of extracting information from people reluctant to part with it. The basis of 1984 was already in place by 1945. The sciences of warfare and surveillance were starting to take priority in the democratic West, and they were not about to take reduced importance in the despotic East. The atomic war of Orwell's tale never happened, but it did not need to, since both sides lived in constant fear that at any moment, it would. And constantly growing was the power of the secretive, cruel, military-corporate state.

Concerning the Cold War, the tide of battle turned in favour of the West with the Berlin Airlift of 1948. Not only was Stalin forced to abandon his siege of West Berlin, stopping his conquests there, but the world saw that the Western powers were willing to risk war in order to safeguard the freedom of an extremely vulnerable outpost. As Orwell observed, the United States had taken over the British Empire. But in those days the United States was a leader, not a ruler, leading in a people-oriented way not seen previously. The British dominions (totally independent since 1917) voluntarily helped people who had been fierce enemies only three years earlier. Even France, Germany's most ardent mortal enemy, gave assistance.

The airlift, in which small numbers of Western forces faced overwhelming numbers on the Soviet side, turned West Berlin into a beacon of unity for free people against Stalinism. It demonstrated to the world (even those behind the Iron Curtain) that the United States was dedicated to the principle of freedom, and was willing to take risks to protect freedom for others, even former enemies. The Soviets, in contrast, came across as bullies of the ancient type, interested only in plundering the lands they had conquered. The Soviets were never able to overcome that public relations defeat, despite many errors on the part of the West, despite efforts by Stalin's successors to change the perception. Since the Cold War was fortunately fought mostly on informational battlegrounds, the Berlin Airlift was a turning point as important as Stalingrad, Midway, or El Alamein in WWII.

The Berlin Airlift ended less than a month before 1984 was published. In the four years between the end of WWII and that time, it looked very much as if Russia would take over all of Europe, with the exception of Airstrip One. The Berlin Airlift changed that scenario, and Europe remained sharply divided between the two super-powers' spheres of influence. The American-controlled half was more valuable industrially, and under U.S. influence Western Europe became a prosperous, powerful, free economic and political bloc, while the areas under Russian sway never fully recovered from the destruction of the war and the piracy committed by the Red Army. Eastern Europe aptly fit Orwell's description of the world of *1984*, "a bare, hungry, dilapidated place" (p. 155) where bomb craters went unfilled, detonated buildings were not rebuilt.

The atomic war (which in Orwell's vision led to the establishment of despotism in the Western democracies) never occurred, so we still maintain some of our liberties. But smaller shocks and many scares since WWII have gradually eroded them all. Throughout the years, the corporate state has gained immense control over our lives. The military-industrial complex has grown more adept at serving its own interests while ignoring the interests of the American people, and the American Empire has become an empire in the traditional sense, employing a lot of pomp and bombast with its big stick, utilizing violence to hold sway over its far-flung subjects. The America whose Commander-in-Chief, Truman, ordered the Berlin Airlift became the America whose Commander-in-Chief, Nixon, attempted to bomb Indo-China "into the Stone Age", within a single generation.

6

Coming to Power

"And at the same time the consequences of being at war, and therefore in danger, makes the handing-over of all power to a small caste seem the natural, unavoidable condition of survival." - *1984*

With admirable craft, the "small caste" of plutocrats took power after the Vietnam fiasco had nearly ruined its well-executed, gradual coup d'etat.   America's military reputation had been reduced to at best a bad joke. The plutocrats' most loyal servants in the Nixon administration had been discredited, even incarcerated, after the Watergate scandals. An opportunity for honest change, for rebuilding our democracy, was there. But within five years, the small caste had retaken power more solidly than before all that trouble had started. While Eisenhower had warned us against the military-industrial complex, Ronald Reagan praised it.

After Vietnam and Watergate, we had the energy crisis, the Soviet invasion of that suddenly important country called Afghanistan, the Iranian hostage crisis, Marxist revolutions in Latin America, industrial decline and economic stagflation. While our problems mounted, many Americans had become so disillusioned with the political process that they withdrew from taking part. Those who remained were dominated by aging, fearful citizens in comfortable circumstances, who thought we would all be better off if we returned to good times before the New Deal. A glorious future would be ours, if we could go back to a halcyon past. The here-and-now was too unpleasant to keep. Ronald Reagan pitched the product well: a country made for rugged individualism, controlled by the self-made men who had already made their way to the top. These were the people who knew best, and there would be no more questioning their wisdom. The Ministry of Truth, headquartered in Madison Avenue, saw to that.

The working classes would need to be divided —the uppity minorities, young people, feminists, and other agitators—from the dear hearts and gentle people who played by the rules, earned their keep, and built this country. This meant for the most part older white men, women who lived with them, and those who could someday be older white men. Reagan was expert at telling these people what they wanted to hear: that they were self-made individualists exactly like the ones who controlled the country. Of course they lacked wealth and power, but they would be the first to be let in, should the elites ever decide they wanted to share. All the while the upper class took more wealth and consolidated more power.

To keep the masses from realizing what was actually happening, the elites need war. But Vietnam had severely dampened Americans' enthusiasm for war. Reagan revived Cold War tensions, and gave us little wars like Grenada to boost our national esteem. During the eighties, the Russians' disaster in Afghanistan was becoming their Vietnam, and the Soviet system, fragile in every way but militarily, began to show serious flaws that the Iron Curtain could no longer hide. In America, the Japanese portion of Eastasia (which a generation earlier had been completely dependent on America for sustenance) was taking over large parts of the U.S. economy. More sacrifices would be necessary.

After the Soviet Union imploded, America was once again psychologically ready for more war. Another little one in Panama (which the elites believed was really an American colony and ought to be grateful for that) was so popular that George Bush I decided it was time for a big war with Iraq. This was paid for by Tokyo and Berlin, and at war's end the American Empire was once again supreme in the world. And like all other empires, The United States of America provided economic benefits to only a small minority at the top. Economic superiority allowed the elites to consolidate political power.

Economic inequality caused a recession soon after, which always happens when workers are unable to buy everything they have produced. "It's the economy, stupid," got Bill Clinton into the White House. A generation earlier, Clinton, a conservative Democrat, would have gotten along quite well with the elites, who knew he would work with them. But by the nineties, the elites' power had grown so immense that they were not interested in working with a president. They demanded that he work for them. And the propaganda machine had become so sophisticated, that the true believers in the Republican Party could be worked into such an anti- Clinton frenzy that they could force Clinton to fight for his political life instead of moving ahead with even minor progressive policies.

Though Clinton was no foe of the military-industrial complex, he knew better than to give it free rein. There were the Balkan Wars, and U.S. planes bombed Iraq, but for the most part we had peace, and a return to some prosperity. To the commoners in the right-wing opposition (who gained economically, just as their forefathers did from the New Deal) Clinton was nevertheless anathema. It made no difference that he was culturally one of them. At the dawn of the new millennium (which many had feared for no reason) half the voters hated him and half were happy with him, while nearly half of the eligible voters were too indifferent to vote. This situation set up the disastrous election of 2000, which was decided by the five openly pro-corporate justices on the Supreme Court.

The Bush-Cheney administration wasted no time returning the country to a war mentality. The Twin Towers explosions were manna from heaven for the military-industrial complex.

Part 2 - Ignorance is Strength

7

Science Lite

"Science, in the old sense, has almost ceased to exist. In Newspeak there is no word for 'Science.' The empirical method of thought, on which all the scientific achievements of the past were founded, is opposed to the most fundamental principles of Ingsoc. And even technological progress only happens when its products can in some way be used for the diminution of human liberty." - *1984*

In the United States of America at the start of the Third Millennium, six centuries after the Renaissance, three into the Enlightenment, nearly as long into the Scientific and Industrial

Revolutions, voters are electing politicians who deny global warming, who advocate teaching creationism in science classes, who direct educators not to teach critical thinking. History is being rewritten, not according to what happened, but to what some elites want us to believe. Again, this is the start of the Third Millennium, not the end of the First. As America's wars in Iraq and Afghanistan wind down and the citizens refuse to pay the price of a new war with Syria, science is giving us the means of killing people with high-tech drones. And the state is acquiring ever more sophisticated means of watching everything we do. Science may not yet be wholly Orwellian, but many influential people are pushing to achieve such a reality.

Big Brother does more than watch us. He can now harass us in ways that once were illegal. Richard Nixon had to resign over conduct that the Patriot Act allows. Some states allow police to determine subjectively if someone looks like an illegal immigrant, to demand the suspect prove his legal status, to arrest him if he cannot. And this can be done to anyone, not only to "those people." Electronic surveillance on the streets and in our homes is on a level of sophistication that makes Orwell's telescreens seem primitive. Torture—now known as "enhanced interrogation", is publicly promoted and supported by large numbers of citizens. The rules of the debate have been twisted to the point that those who would eliminate torture cannot argue on the basis of its cruelty or illegality in international law—they must argue only on the basis of its usefulness, and the burden of proof is on the anti-torturers. Again, we have reached an Orwellian state of mind where torture, which was once roundly condemned, has become accepted, even cheered, as long as it is done to the enemy.

Ignorance: the conscious refusal to confront and examine reality, is practiced by many Americans. It brings a level of strength to those who promote it. It is a strength based on fear and resulting anger, strength of safety in numbers, of circling the wagons against savage outsiders, of a gang brutally pounding its adversaries. It is the strength of bullies, of mobs, and it endows the fearful with a false sense of security that never abolishes fear. It is not real strength, the deep-seated strength that sustains humans in times of stress and crisis. It is the strength that the power-hungry cultivate in those they would rule. If it ever emerges as the dominant emotion in our culture, the best advise is: never murmur "down with Big Brother" in your sleep.

8

Insisting upon Ignorance

"Science investigates, religion interprets. Science gives man knowledge, which is power. Religion gives man wisdom, which is control. Science deals mainly with facts; religion deals mainly with values. The two are not rivals." - Martin Luther King, Jr.

When Mitt Romney, the Republican nominee for president in 2012, makes a joke about global warming, and his audience laughs raucously, we can safely bet that denial is profitable. Since the late sixties the party of denial has probably won more elections than it has lost, and in large parts of the country it holds firm control. The rival party has admitted global warming, but in a half-hearted way, trying to play down the needed solutions, lest the mob rise in fear of change, and further empower the deniers. Ignorance is strength for the elites who control the main cause of global warming, the burning of fossil fuels. These elites could promote knowledge and lead the way to solutions to global warming, using their money and business acumen to develop alternative clean, renewable energy production, which would enhance their profits. But new energy sources would also probably enrich everyone, and currently the elites have a lock on profits, and so have a lock on power as well. And as O'Brien says: "God is Power."

True believers seem to be attracted to creeds that make little if any sense, as we have seen throughout history. Such creeds, impervious to reason, create formidable adversaries to anyone who would oppose them. Hence, science is ignored in the case of global warming, and the elites, few in number, who profit immensely from mankind's dependence on fossil fuels, are able to maintain control by firing up the impassioned mob. Rational people are at a disadvantage.

Jokes about global warming make it clear that reasoned argument has no place among true believers.

In a democracy the majority is theoretically persuaded to make rational choices because people have the freedom to choose. One half the usual voters in the United States have chosen to stand firm against rational choices, purposely ignoring threats to their existence. The one percent who have been using the willfully ignorant to their own ends know better. Only loyalty to a deity such as power explains this situation.

The appeal for those who render power to the corporate elite, against their self-interest, has no reasonable explanation. Perhaps simply having to change is frightening enough to shut out all new information. The world is changing rapidly, in every possible way, which bothers everyone living on this planet. For some, the bother is too painful to address, so denial is the first option. Denial is encouraged and enforced with unlimited funds to buy most of the media and overwhelm the society with corporate propaganda. The corporate state overseeing this propaganda barrage becomes dictatorial in time, but it cannot establish itself. It comes about because people—not necessarily a majority—want it. There is no thought behind this desire, only an aversion to the way things are going.

Most people everywhere are content to work for a living, raise families, enjoy friends, and have some harmless fun. We like to leave one another alone, and be left alone. Scientific information, in the case of global warming, appears to demand changes in our lifestyles. Collective solutions to everyone's problem can look frightening. And there is always the chance that the solutions will not work. Perhaps they really are not necessary. Most people, while welcoming mild changes for the better and accepting mild changes for the worse, are daunted by major changes. There are always people who will take advantage of these fears, and we are in a period when these opportunists happen to be our society's rulers. Their control of information is formidable.

Still, the truth is available, if we would face it. The modern plutocracy has not yet realized complete censorship. Rationalizations, jokes, and denial cannot change reality, but it is up to us who see the reality to point it out. Oddly, the right wing's resistance to change is more dangerous to the status quo than making appropriate changes in our economic system. We who accept scientific reality and the need for collective solutions have no choice but to present the evidence, to tell the truth. The hardcore deniers are probably incapable of perceiving the truth. But there are many whose minds are still open. These are the ones to be informed. Ignorance is no longer a universal condition of mankind. We choose it.

9

Setting Sun

"All rulers of all ages have tried to impose a false view of the world upon their followers, but they could not afford to encourage any illusion that tended to impair military efficiency. So long as defeat meant the loss of independence, or some other result generally held to be undesirable, the precautions against defeat had to be serious. Physical facts could not be ignored." - *1984*

Ronald Reagan had workers remove solar panels from the White House, which had been installed during Jimmy Carter's administration. Scarcely marked at the time, this event was significant, as it meant the presidential energy priorities would remain dependent on fossil fuels. It was one way of saying that the government would have no energy policy, real or symbolic, and that the "magic of the marketplace" would decide how America fueled its industry, business, and lifestyle. Of course the marketplace was rigged to benefit the fossil fuel producers, who also happened to be large contributors to politicians like Reagan. But since Reagan won both his presidential elections by landslides, it was plain that most Americans were not interested in change either. While free markets and rugged individualism were the pretty packages dressing up Reagan's energy policy (claiming no policy is still a policy), what was left unsaid was that the ruling clique of the United States was confident that its territorial integrity would be preserved.

By the eighties, the three super-states: America, Russia, and China, corresponding with Oceania, Eurasia, and Eastasia, had been established, and it was generally understood that each was invincible. Each power was too big to be conquered by foreign invasion, and each had nuclear weapons, which rendered the territorial frontiers of each invulnerable to attack. The resulting situation made possible a truly Orwellian consolidation of power for the rulers of each super-state. In America the elites embraced the opportunity. Their agents moved to consolidate control of the economy, which meant controlling energy distribution, which incidentally meant stifling scientific inquiry in order to preserve the dominance of fossil fuels.

Real or potential advantages of renewable energy sources being no longer essential to national survival, the ruling clique could do without investing in these ventures, which let the rulers keep more profits. In reality, if clean, permanent energy could be developed on a large scale, the economic advantages would raise everyone's standard of living. Elites do not want this, because their power depends on economic inequality. The workers must demand greater equality, if they want it. Most workers, for whatever reasons, voted for Reagan, and he took down the solar panels. "Give me a solar generator the size of a cornfield, and I'll run your portable radio till the sun goes down," went the old joke. Of course new energy sources were famously inefficient and prohibitively expensive, and Reagan's non-policy meant for them to stay that way. If somebody could come up with efficient renewable energy, that was fine, but he would do it without any help from government.

Doublethink (or "reality control" in Oldspeak) allows the corporate rulers, and their subjects, to ignore the fact that business has, since America's founding, thrived with government help. Though at some times government leaders have disagreed with business leaders, at no time has the U.S. government been hostile to business. Fossil fuel producers have manipulated the political, legal, informational, and economic segments of our society to the point where they enjoy great advantages courtesy of government. Yet they can still claim to be "self-made men."

The combination of business finesse and government facilitation made life, for most Americans, reasonably provident—enviably so after WWII. Problems arose in the 1960's and 1970's, when social, economic, and political controversies made our everyday prosperity seem less secure than we had grown used to believing. Changes appeared uncomfortably close, and

Americans were uncomfortable accepting them. Ronald Reagan assured Americans that would not be necessary. America the powerful would convince the world to respect us. Reports have surfaced that Edwin Meese, Reagan's right-hand man, felt that solar water heaters were beneath the dignity of a superpower. A president's shower should be warmed with oil from Persian Gulf client states.

In a logical universe, forced reliance on dirty, exhaustible, unreliable power sources would be hard to explain. In the 1980's global warming was not widely known, but the other dangers of pollution were. Calling for nationwide efforts to achieve energy independence, Carter hoped to summon the "moral equivalent of war." He summoned reactions from polite indifference to derisive ridicule. The right-wing vehemently decried any and all government-sponsored programs as wasteful, ineffective, and dictatorial. Reagan repeated his claim that only the free market, without governmental regulation, could reliably assure plentiful energy.

Furthermore, argued Reagan and his supporters, Carter's plans, emphasizing public works and conservation, would actually impede real solutions to the energy crisis. Only by going ahead, using energy as we always had, could American know-how be unleashed to solve the problem. Pollution, though rumoured to be caused by burning fossil fuels, was actually caused by trees, Reagan assured us. So we would do well to cut down as many of those as we could. If solar, wind, biomass, geyser, and other "exotic" energy sources could compete on an open market, good. But they would need to compete fairly, against the fossil and nuclear giants, who would keep their subsidies, tax loopholes, regulatory advantages, access to resources, and friendly politicians. As we know, Reagan won the 1980 election.

Reagan's policies, by ignoring science, in effect set the stage for the global climate crisis we face a generation later. He could ignore scientific innovations because his backers among the corporate elite and the military-industrial complex knew they were invulnerable to foreign conquest.
The same group is still in charge. The same group still denies the existence of global warming, and fiercely resists attempts to

remedy the problem. Carter's attempt to muster a "moral equivalent of war" to solve the energy crisis in the seventies was in vain. By the early nineties, George Bush I addressed the energy crisis by going to war in Iraq, an action imitated by Bush II some twelve years later.

10

Rising Star

"The scientist of today is either a mixture of psychologist and inquisitor, studying with extraordinary minuteness the meaning of facial expressions, gestures, and tones of voice, and testing the truth-producing effects of drugs, shock therapy, and physical torture; or he is a chemist, physicist, or biologist, concerned only with such branches of his special subject as are relevant to the taking of life." - *1984*

There is no denying the tremendous advantages for all mankind, of the agreements made between the super-powers to forego nuclear war, and to try to prevent other nations from waging it. Grateful as we all should be at the lessening of nuclear tensions, we are now obliged to examine where we stand in relation to our leadership. Since Russia, China, and the United States (with or without their bordering empires) are too big to be conquered by foreign invasion, and have agreed not to attack one another with nuclear weapons, the ruling elites of each super-power are invulnerable from without. Now their concern is to prevent any threats from within. The rulers of each have effectively eliminated this main threat, from a rising middle class, by eliminating their middle classes. Science has solved many problems for all humanity in the past two centuries, and science, used wisely, could solve many more. But solutions would have to include poverty and privation, and eliminating these would end income inequality, which the elites in each sphere depend on to maintain power.

The global warming issue is an outstanding example of how the world's rulers have tacitly agreed to ignore a threat to humanity's well-being, if not existence. The fact is that the elites could retain power in a climate crisis, whereas solving the crisis would probably end their economic superiority, and so, their power. The rulers of each super-state have found they can communicate and conduct commerce with each other and still keep power, which on the surface appears to discredit Orwell's theory. Actually, cooperation between the rulers reduces the possibility of misunderstandings, which could lead to that now improbable nuclear showdown. Cooperation between super-states in defiance of climate science has reached ultimate irony with the selling of American coal to China, a commercial venture that makes no sense from any standpoint but profit for the traders involved.

Capitalism holds sway, in the three super-states, and worldwide. Russia replaced its tired Bolshevik bureaucracy with plutocracy, to the enrichment of former communist bureaucrats. The Red Chinese have traded their peasant garb for western-style suits. Apparently "free enterprise" is more marketable than "workers' revolution". But the results are, in all super-states, corporate control of internal doings: fascism. The extent of the rule by the elites is in the three super-states softer than Orwell predicted—somewhere between "thou shalt not" and "thou shalt". The insistence on "thou art" exists only in the corporate boardrooms, but the mechanisms for complete control are available in all super-states to be used everywhere, should the elites ever need them.

While electronic surveillance of individual actions has surpassed the nightmares described by Orwell, the search for the ultimate weapon goes on quietly. Ronald Reagan's "Star Wars" boondoggle stands out as a famous example of the ruling class's successful campaign to squelch movements for real peace. While the project never worked, it did manage to stop a growing peace movement in its tracks. With détente between America's two communist rivals reducing the nuclear annihilation threat, some citizens actually began to envision world peace. People worldwide began to realize how much in common they all had. Grassroots movements began to seriously question the direction the world had been taking since the end of WWII. Revivals of peace and resistance movements seemed eminent. For the elites, these events were a threat. Détente was one thing, but an end to all wars was entirely different. Fortunately for the elites, Reagan was president.

Reagan was blessed, or cursed, with the ability to believe his own tall tales, which played well on TV and accounted for his success. When he came out with his proposal for a missile defense shield, he presented a pretty picture of the elimination of all possibility of nuclear war. The idea, at first glance, was sublime: no need to trust foreigners by making treaties. This ultimate weapon would make war impossible by making guided missiles obsolete. In truth, this ultimate weapon would insure superiority for the United States, and these implications convinced most of the media establishment to support Reagan's proposal. Liberal commentators claimed the anti-missile missile had been tried before and failed. Reagan countered with the "good old Yankee ingenuity" argument, saying all we needed was faith in our country's spirit and ability. Many Americans believed him. The formerly discredited military-industrial complex had been completely vindicated, and was once more all that kept us from communist slavery. Officially labeled the "Strategic Defense Initiative," Reagan's plan was called "Star Wars" by its detractors. Reagan reminded everyone "the Force is with Us."

The scheme, which basically consisted of computerized satellites which could detect missiles anywhere, and could send laser beams out to destroy any missile upon launching, has never, in thirty years, come close to actuality. Still, being announced in 1983, it shows us how Orwell's scenario kept to schedule. Reagan pitched it as a system that would end the threat of nuclear warfare, but this wonderful future would only happen if the other nuclear powers would unconditionally surrender. After all, everyone would still have nuclear weapons, but only America would be able to launch them. Victory would go to the good guys, unless the bad guys built the system first, which increased the urgency for our side to tighten our belts and get to work. Like it or not, more money would need to go to military expenses.

As a technology, the Star Wars project was a failure, and quickly forgotten. However, it served its true purpose: to destroy the viability of the peace movement and shore up the military-industrial complex. It ruined any chance we had then for achieving real peace, and allowed the rulers to go on waging small, far-off, yet expensive wars. The populace was "educated" to accept ongoing war, so the elites, freed from outside threats, could deal with the three internal threats to their power: a strong Middle, revolt of the masses, or elites' loss of their own confidence. The elites' ability to resist or pre-empt these threats depend on the strength of ignorance to perpetuate war as peace.

11

Death and Opportunity

"At the apex of the pyramid comes Big Brother. Big Brother is infallible and all-powerful....We may be reasonably sure that he will never die..." - *1984*

"A movement is pioneered by men of words, materialized by fanatics, and consolidated by men of action." - Erich Hoffer, *The True Believer*

Ronald Reagan is as close to a Big Brother type as we have yet in the United States. Fortunately, though he was a charismatic president, he never attained that level of perception as being all-knowing, which assures us that we still have the liberty of honest disagreement, difficult as that disagreement might sometimes be in practice. Nonetheless, our concept of free society needs considerable reinforcement. In their respective super-states, Stalin and Mao came much closer to fitting the Big Brother role than Reagan, yet both have been disappeared, mainly due to the fact that being human, they died. Orwell, who died three years before "Uncle Joe" Stalin, was unable to make observations on how modern dictator-ships transfer power. Hitler, Tojo, and Mussolini were probably the last great power autocrats to be replaced by foreign invaders. Orwell had no way of knowing how modern heirs to despots manage the changeover. It turns out that Stalin's heirs had no interest in keeping him alive.

The main problem with perpetuating someone's life after his death stems from a general perception of reality. Even masses who have been swindled, starved, trampled, murdered, evicted, imprisoned, and otherwise denied all trappings of civilization, are sophisticated enough to know that death is universal. Even Jesus of Nazareth, the only founder of a mass movement who is believed to have survived phys-ical death, needed to be murdered before he could be miraculously revived. Then he, too, went the "way of all flesh." In the atheistic states of the modern era, it is commonly held that life exists only on this planet, between birth and death. In Russia, which had undergone nothing but mass death for thirty-nine years prior to Stalin's passing, it would be expected that even the revered "Uncle" must die.

Stalin's successors were human too, so it stands to reason they would want him dead. They had endured endless purges, watching others disappear while each wondered if he might be next. They had spent their lifetimes towing the party line, changing each time the line changed, while hoping no one would notice that they remembered what it had previously been. Asleep or awake, they had tried to anticipate what "Uncle Joe" might be thinking next, to think the same thing the moment he did. In a world in which betray or be betrayed was the key to advancement, even survival, in which no human goals other than to please "Uncle Joe" were left, those commissars who survived Stalin would have no desire to keep him around.

Merely three years after Stalin's death, Kruschev made him an unperson.

For thirty-five more years, the Soviet Empire staggered along, while the ruling clique tried to fix Stalinism. But the mortal wounds endured by Russians since 1914 needed more than a systemic fix. Despite rigid censorship, Soviet subjects found out that people lived much better on the other side of the Iron Curtain. By 1991 the ruling clique had lost confidence. In a relatively quiet revolt, the middle class, mainly lower-ranking Party operatives, took control, broke up the Soviet Empire, and joyfully embraced plutocracy. The rulers of America, taking no chances that Russia might actually implement honest social democracy, invited the newly freed Soviet colonies into NATO, thus assuring Russians that they were still the enemy, which assisted the transition from communism to corporate rule.

China's transition from Maoist fanaticism to a tightly controlled corporate state was even smoother than Russia's. At any rate, Chinese workers have plenty of work (at low pay) and the "practical men of action" who now rule have not officially renounced Marxism. With cosmetic differences relating to the cultures of Russia and China, both super-states have become examples of the evil that Marxism opposed.

From an Orwellian standpoint, the insanity needed to maintain paranoid absolute power has been set aside for a guaranteed level of softer, but still total, power. Whether these events mean the pendulum will swing again, that the Uppers will once more liberalize and so lose power to a ruthless Middle, remains part of a wide-open field of speculation. Tensions between authoritarianism and republicanism are always evolving, and we update our speculations as events unfold. From "the end of the Neolithic Age" until the Renaissance (5,000 to 6,000 years) very little changed in the real lives of humans. Things changed radically from the Renaissance to the time of *1984*'s publication, and we know the pace of change since then continues to increase. Orwell (1949) and Hoffer (1951) could only guess at the future based on their observations of the present. We are under the same restrictions and obligations. We need to be aware of reality, so that we see where we might be heading, in order to work together to change directions.

The rulers of China and Russia in the early twenty-first century are hardnosed policy wonks whose prime goal is to get things done. Though they have softened slightly in their intolerance of opposition, they still brook no real challenge to their power, no matter how small. Though the current holders of power refrain from using the extremely brutal methods of their predecessors, this is because the extremes seem not to be necessary. They are still available, and even here in America, we have been selectively employing dictatorial means of coercion since the fall of the Twin Towers in 2001.

China's and Russia's ruling cliques have morphed into the same corporate-government partnership that dominates America: Mussolini's definition of fascism. The rulers of each compete for resources and profits, but they do not threaten each others' power. All rule efficiently enough to keep the masses placid, and rigidly enough to frighten the masses into accepting their lot. All maintain rigid dominance over the middle class, which is now their primary goal, since none can be conquered from outside.

Many thoughtful, intelligent, educated people believe strong top-down government to be the best government in all ways, that those who have greatest wealth have the largest stake in preserving peace and stability. Many are also somehow convinced that corporate domination of government will in time eliminate the need for government altogether, or at least make government "small enough to strangle in the bathtub," as Grover Norquist claims to fervently hope. They clearly believe their creed, despite evidence of climate catastrophe, and of ecological disaster even if the climate remains stable; of billions living in poverty although our ability to distribute goods and services is more efficient than it ever has been—all clear evidence of doublethink in action.

More devastating to mankind's mental health than material poverty and environmental destruction, is the eradication of traditional social systems, of individuals' sense of belonging in the world. When people are cast adrift from long-time social moorings, they are ripe for revivals of fanaticism, and the atrocities that fanatics, who feel they are always right, believe they have the right to commit. And nothing eviscerates social traditions as completely as corporate power.

A wild card is introduced into the scenario with mass electronic communication. Currently, elites have access to the details of everyone's lives, but (as the Manninng and Snowden revelations tell) they also have no secrets from the rest of us. Information is exchanged instantly and universally, and this goes on with little control from anyone. The imperfections of public figures are well known to all. Of course the elites find this situation unsatisfactory, and they strive constantly to regain their monopoly of information. They could simply overwhelm all other information, as they are doing thanks to the blessing given them by the Supreme Court in Citizens' United. This would be much cheaper than installing more Gulags, with the added benefit of preserving the illusion of freedom of speech. Power of the ruling elites would be preserved, without the need to apply new coats of paint to Big Brother's image.

12

The More Things Change

"But in matters of vital importance—meaning, in effect, war and police espionage—the empirical approach is still encouraged, or at least tolerated." - *1984*

"If the president can order the killing of American citizens abroad should he decide they are involved with Al Qaeda, can he assassinate suspected Al Qaeda-connected US citizens in London or Berlin? - Katha Pollitt, *The Nation*, March. 4, 2013

Pollitt's question answers itself: of course. In the never-ending war with Al Qaeda (have we not always been at war with Al Qaeda?) we must do all we can to achieve final victory, setting aside the fact that we also know final victory over every potential terrorist is impossible. Bombing our long-time friends' capitals would be politically messy, but war is never neat, never moral. Drone technology offers us the illusion (like "smart bombs" previously) that we can now bomb only bad guys. It allows us the illusion that we now possess that ultimate weapon. In a mechanical sense we have come full circle, back to the V-1 and V-2 rockets that incessantly fell on London in WWII, that were still falling everywhere on Airstrip One in Orwell's dystopia. Keeping with the Orwellian theme, our government proudly displays our supreme craft in developing these weapons, while government tries at the same time to stifle the spread of scientific research when it comes to climate or evolution.

Hitler resorted to rockets because the allied Air Forces had decimated Germany's. The United States still has a supreme Air Force, but from the standpoint of the corporate, military-industrial State, unmanned delivery of explosives has become necessary. Two long wars having reduced the American public's tolerance of war to virtually zero, the State must now perpetuate its war while eliminating the perception of Americans' participation in it. Though American casualties in our Middle Eastern wars have been small by modern standards, electronic media have made those casualties personal, and the moment that war casualties become known and felt on the part of the civilian population, war ceases to be peace. With drones we can once more enjoy the satisfaction of killing the bad guys, without fear of retribution. Once more we are tempted to embrace the insane notion that we can win a war. We forget that no ultimate weapon has ever remained long in the arsenal of only one nation. Drones will be imitated.

The prospect of eternal war, with all sides sending drones overseas to destroy random targets (as Orwell predicts) is terrifying, but drone technology also opens up the equally frightening prospect of drone surveillance of everyone and everything, all the time. The scientific method is being used to develop the same technology for the Uppers' major goal: perpetuating their power through incessant war and incessant observation of the people. Many citizens are justifiably upset by these developments, while spokespersons for the corporate state treat them as a fait accompli, scarcely worth our notice in these busy times. In American politics, one party uses drones to kill even American citizens, at will. The other party applauds this practice, and would also take away our Medicare and Social Security. In official circles the supremacy of the military-industrial complex is assumed.

The result, based on history, will be a world in which all major nations and most minor ones have drones. For the elites rulling the super powers the danger of all-out drone warfare to their power will become obvious. Use of drones will be curtailed, with or without treaties. However, the desired objective: using up surplus production without raising the general standard of living, will be achieved. In the primitive, dysfunctional parts of the world, those eternal colonies, drones will still be purchased and used, giving scientists real-life experiments to improve the technology. And drone surveillance of citizens will be here to stay.

And we will have squandered another opportunity to stop war from being peace.

Part 3 - Freedom is Slavery

13

A Paen to the Proles

"If there is hope (wrote Winston) it lies in the proles." - *1984*

"Those who own the country, ought to govern it." -John Jay, *The Federalist,* 1787-88

No one seriously believes that the party structure described by Orwell exists in the United States. However, the fact that we have never come close to a hierarchy of Inner Party, Outer Party, and Proletariat does not mean our democracy is safe. The superficial front of a classless society (we have no idea who might grow rich, therefore we are encouraged to believe anyone can get rich) scarcely hides the reality that we live in a constant state of class warfare, that the class warfare is waged by the upper class against the other two, and the fact only becomes evident when the lower classes begin to fight back.

As Orwell points out, the Upper remains in power by controlling the Middle. The Middle has its best chance of replacing the Upper by enlisting the Lower to side with it, promising equality. The historical reality holds true even without the terrifying Stalinist features Orwell grafts onto Western society. The ruling elites in America stay in power by economic policies designed to render the middle class powerless and poor. These policies have been enormously successful over the past thirty or forty years. The capitalists ruling our country need not use Stalinist cruelty to disable the middle class. Layoffs, foreclosures, bankruptcies, union-busting and threats to confiscate pensions keep us fearful. The refusal of half the elected politicians to do anything about it, and the inability of the other half to overcome the inertia, have been as effective at retaining power as telescreens, two-minute hates, and Room 101. People in what once was the middle class are fearful, suspicious, distrustful of one another. As the bones dangled before them grow scrawnier and fewer, they fight harder for what bones remain. The middle class has been lumped in with the working poor, the class once known as the proletariat, and in this condition they are hard-put to fight together for a better life.

Beginning with the end of WWII, the blending of middle class and proletariat was proceeding in the other direction, toward a strong and prosperous giant middle class. Factory work and work in the trades became more cerebral, requiring more education. Government enacted legislation to ensure greater economic security and unions promoted higher living standards for everyone. Higher education was readily available for many. Furthermore, society was moving in a direction that promised more of the same. This resulted in a blurring of class lines. Great wealth was possible for more people of the middle and even lower classes, and those who did not get rich could live well. Times were not perfect. There were still recessions and stubborn pockets of poverty even in the Land of Plenty. Individuals could still make unfortunate choices, lose jobs, and grow poor. But life for most was good, and promised credibly to get better. It was possible to believe that America truly was the land of opportunity, that we had achieved a classless society.

At the end of the Iraq War, the scene is different. The gap between rich and poor having expanded to pre-Depression era levels, the rich have regained solid control. Politicians who disbelieve in global warming, who promote teaching The Bible as science, who intend to eliminate health care for millions and to privatize Social Security, are in a dead heat with Barack Obama, a moderate to conservative politician who has no intention of upsetting the current power structure, but only of making it more comfortable for the many who are miserable. Like Franklin Roosevelt, Obama seeks to alleviate some of the suffering for the lower classes in hopes of preventing their revolting. Right-wing politicians in modern times, having no fear of the middle class or the proles, see no need to compromise.

The current situation favours the upper class. About half the usual voters (for reasons of their own) support a corporate-run, authoritarian society. The other half is mildly to adamantly opposed. These two groups together form only a little more than half the Americans who could vote. The vast number who claim to have no interest in the outcome of this struggle are the modern "proles" or working poor, although as workers they are becoming obsolete. With their livelihoods shipped overseas to be performed by virtual slaves, they find fewer and fewer jobs, with decreased pay, increased hours, and vaporized pensions and benefits. And though these people benefit more directly from the much-frayed safety net than anyone else, they are unready to do anything to strengthen that net.

Proles cannot be bothered to vote. If they would vote (and like most people vote their self-interests) the elites would be forced to make many compromises. These compromises would materially benefit rich, middle, and poor alike, but they would effectively eliminate the current situation in which the upper one percent exercise true power over everyone else. Understandably the one percent are interested in keeping the proles from voting. In the 2012 election, many of the working poor did go to the polls, despite determined efforts in several states to make their voting so difficult as to be not worth the trouble. Political machines serving the plutocracy are redoubling their efforts to restrict or eliminate voting in poor neighbourhoods. At the same time, advocates for the disenfranchised are increasing their efforts to encourage the poor to vote, to make it easier for them to do so. The fight is on.

The proles are stirring. Whether they actually wake up remains yet to be seen, but restoring our ravaged democracy depends on their doing so. With the Middle and the Lower compressed actually into one economic unit, we have a rare opportunity for members of both to recognize their common needs and act upon them. As we learn from O'Brien's boastful rants about the impossibility of the proles ever rising up, Orwell is cynical. The cynicism is justified, yet the opportunity is present.

Many of us know something is wrong, that we are being lied to, played for suckers. We are like Winston Smith, clinging to that slip of news that proved The Party had lied about Aaronson, Jones, and Rutherford, vaporized Party leaders accused of high treason. We are numbered among the brutalized middle class and the educated working poor, distinctions that grow less obvious every day. There are definitely two classes now: the elites and everyone else, and we who know are obliged to raise the awareness of others. Right now, all proles are robbed, but many do not know it. Due to fear, the load of poverty, or chronic denial, many of them resist awareness. But if there is hope, it lies in them. If they do not waken and fight back, they are, by a twisted definition, free as animals. So: "Freedom is Slavery."

14

You Are Free—Now Back to Work

"The unavoidable conclusion seems to be that when the individual faces torture or annihilation, he cannot rely on the resources of his own individuality." - Eric Hoffer, *The True Believer*

Exceptional individuals throughout history have had difficulty staying out of prison and avoiding execution. The Age of Enlightenment, by introducing the concept of the importance of all individuals, sought the betterment of society by recognizing that some individuals have foresight the rest of us do not, and that we should listen to them. Since then the race has moved, haltingly, to realize individualism as a mainstay in a healthy society. In word, if not in deed, the individual is revered. Despots who try to silence those who challenge their power must come up with excuses now, such as "law and order" or "troubled times"—quite a change from just a few centuries ago, when displeasing the Divine Right monarch for any reason was an unquestioned capital offense.

The founding fathers of the United States were Enlightenment men, who number among their handiwork two of the Enlightenment's most important documents: The *Declaration of Independence* and the U.S. *Constitution*. Both documents sought to incorporate into law the greatest potential for individual expression and achievement for "All men," who "are created equal." At the time "All men" referred to white males with some property: the Middle, which had just replaced the Upper (the British nobility). Still, the equality issue was for the first time stated openly,which left the door ajar, if ever so slightly, for everyone else. From 1776 on, the burden of proof would be on anyone who would exclude some people from full participation in society's doings.

Since that time the course of human progress has moved toward inclusion for all individuals. Progress has been notoriously irregular, often bloody, and at certain times in many places it looked to be backsliding into worse repression and inequality than before. Still the general trend of history has been toward a reality of equality for "all men."

Understandably, trends are meaningless to people who are hungry, whose children die from treatable illnesses, who are imprisoned for their beliefs, who are blown apart for the profit of strangers—the list seems endless. We may be created equal, but fellow humans are always seeking to undo that creation. To some people, in many respects, O'Brien's "boot stomping on a human face" is the future. Whether it be forever, not even O'Brien can accurately predict, but it seems like forever to anyone whose face is under that boot. Economic and social chaos can lead to political authoritarianism. Perceiving this, the founding fathers sought to enhance the prospect of individual wellbeing by forming "a more perfect union." They understood that hyper-competition between individuals could lead to the ultimate triumph of one. They foresaw Napoleon.

The founders, seeking through the *Declaration of Independence* the recognition of their equality with George III, recognized that with their equal rights went equal responsibilities. Their next document opened with "We the People", which acknowledged that equal individuals must work together to "secure the blessings of liberty." The relative good fortune of the United States is due in large part to the fact that the founding fathers, looking out for their enlightened self-interest, took power and almost immediately began to open the door for sharing power. Aware that by seizing power they would naturally face challenges to their rule, they wrote into their second Enlightenment document mechanisms to maintain their primacy while enabling others to make changes. This document, which became the Law of the Land, provided for eventual expansion of those eligible to participate in the governing process and allowed for some fluidity between the classes.

Those who had the money still had the advantages, but among the founders the desire to protect their own newfound equality and liberty led some of them to consider granting the same to others—under the right conditions. These founders formed the Republican Party, which morphed into the Democratic Party. Other founders, having ascended to primacy, wanted to keep it that way. These were the Federalists, whose party disappeared after a secession attempt during the War of 1812, but emerged a few years later as the Whigs, who also died out, being re-incarnated later as the Republican Party. The first to be let into the new nation's governing process were poor white men. African slaves, Indians, and women, (a partial list) were not considered by either side until much later. To this day both parties are financed by the elites, whose interests they represent, and their differences are similar to those the founders had between their factions. Now that political participation has been extended to all races and both sexes, the struggle is over social and economic equality. The modern Republicans want to retain exclusive domination in the social and economic fields, while Democrats believe order can be more reliably maintained by sharing some of these.

A populist wing wields some influence in the Democratic Party, though it is still subservient to the elitists in the centrist wing. The Republican Party has seen its membership shrink over the same issue that caused the Federalists and Whigs to implode: who is to share in the "blessings of liberty"? Republicans are left with the tiny number of elites, who hold loose control over a base known as the "Tea Party"—composed mainly of older, white males, who insist on retaining social and economic superiority over everyone else. These are the political descend- ants of the "know-nothings" of the mid-nine- teenth century, and the "lunatic fringe" of the late nineteenth and early twentieth. These working class Republicans would have faded into the background but for the support they get from elites such as the Koch Brothers, who manipulate Tea Party voters to take complete power for the elites. Whether the elites can keep control over this modern lunatic fringe is speculative.

Wealthy Germans thought they could control the Nazis, too.

Freedom is always at risk. Both sides have stolen elections. We depend on enlightened self-interest to keep the system working more or less fairly, over time. We do kindly unto others because we do not want them to treat us badly. When one party attempts to game the system unfairly because it does not hope to win elections with fair debate of the issues, those who would preserve liberty can only preserve it by combining forces. "We the People" still need to work together to enhance our personal freedom; else the most rugged individualists among us will lie, cheat, and kill their way to power.

15

Going Around Channels

"In reality very little was known about the Proles. It was not necessary to know much." - *1984*

In 2012, ballot measures in Long Beach and San Jose, California were passed, increasing minimum wages. Unions, having been stymied in work places and in local, state and federal legislative bodies, went directly to voters to get better working conditions. The initiative process, which had been for many years controlled by elites, could be used to do what had been virtually impossible: to actually help working people. But social progress depends upon mathematics

—the ballot measures passed because more workers voted. Other municipalities have seen the same events unfold, and for the same reason. If workers (especially the working and idle poor) voted in large numbers, American society would be basically progressive and egalitarian. Plutocracy and inequality, the pier blocks of the Corporate State, have thrived due to consistently dismal voter turnouts in American elections. The ruling elites have strong incentives to keep large numbers of voters apathetic. And when the people who traditionally ignore elections actually do vote, the hirelings of the power structure work hard to restrict voting in poor neighbourhoods.

Rational people have a healthy fear of mob rule, which explains the founders' efforts to restrict the commoners' access to government. When John Jay wrote "Those who own the country, ought to govern it," he was merely expressing the general view of his peers. Among the Middle who had recently become the Upper in the new nation, it was accepted that some men by nature are more equal than others. Mature people accept that life is unfair, that the talents some possess will be more enriching and empowering than those of others. At the same time, the founders knew they had committed to the principle of equality, of the endowed rights of life, liberty, and the pursuit of happiness, and this was the stated purpose of the new nation's existence. Some among the new elites would naturally seek out ways to guarantee those rights to all.

Having the permission and the resources for self-improvement are all the vast majority of humans ask of their society. Anyone willing to shoulder the burden and responsibility of governing is entitled to fair compensation, as in any other job, and few would grudge him that. Even modest amounts of unfair advantage will be tolerated by most as simply not worth the trouble. The *Declaration of Independence* accepts "…that mankind are more disposed to suffer, while evils are sufferable, than to right themselves by abolishing the forms to which they are accustomed." For some years now, commoners have allowed financial inequality to prevail and increase, doing the best they could with what they could get. This situation may be reaching the limits of toleration.

Beginning in the sixties, and accelerating in the eighties, economic and social inequality have come to define reality in America. The "Great Middle Class," which we were so proud of in the fifties and early sixties, has been gradually locked out of power and denied economic improvement, to the point where abject poverty for most workers is but a downturn or medical problem away. Worker productivity increases while workers see no return for their gains, either in wages or time. Bankruptcies, foreclosures, and mass impoverishment have been scarcely abated through the last three election cycles. Politicians who make even feeble attempts to reduce the suffering and restart the economy meet stark resistance from the servants of the plutocracy. Government function is slowed to a halt while the real economic problems of millions are ignored and allowed to worsen. But the Proles are awakening, as the pro-union elections attest.

There is no doubt that most Americans want to keep Social Security and Medicare; to tax capital gains as income, eliminate offshore tax shelters, and increase taxes on wealth; to make it easier for people to join unions and to vote. This is but a partial list what Americans want by way of government services to help society to function. Yet elected politicians are unable (or unwilling, the debate goes on) to deliver the mundane operations of a sensible government. And the wealthy thrive. Are these daily realities hallmarks of democracy, or indications of budding fascism?

The California pro-union elections show that the working poor and the middle class are beginning to identify with each other, which is only natural, since both groups have been treated harshly over the past forty-plus years by policies that have so heavily favoured the rich. In fact, the two groups have always had much in common: their members have to work for a living. It is true that ethnic and cultural differences hide the similarities, and are used, quite successfully, by the rulers to divide and conquer. Still, the reality is dawning on many who do not belong to that ruling class, that we are being robbed, and we have the means to fight back, democratically and peacefully, if we have the will to do so. There is no chance for success of the working class without collective action. Rugged individualists can expect ruthless treatment from those who are far more rugged.

The wealthy one percent still control the channels of public information, and they have the resources (along with permission to use their resources courtesy of the Supreme Court) to bury all opposition. They could get us into another war, which always makes dissent hard if not impossible. Voters could be lulled into cynicism, which is always tempting, considering the current situation in politics: the servants of the plutocracy refuse to compromise with anything proposed by Barack Obama, a president whose moderation is frustrating to his supporters. Voter restrictions could disenfranchise enough people to swing close elections. Dissent and fear could be sown into the ranks of the workers, so they vote against each others' (and their own) common interests—which has happened often enough to encourage the elites to keep trying. What we know is that the more people vote, the more likely people are to get what they want from their elected politicians. When turnout is light, the servants of the one percent tend to win elections, and with every win, they work diligently to cement their power.

Democracy—rule by people—requires participation from people, or it will not function. We cannot wind it up and walk away. For all its popularity, democracy has had little actual practice in human affairs. After its invention and limited practice in Athens, it lay dormant until writers of the Enlightenment proposed its revival. It has been attempted many times, in many places since, but only in a few locations has it been modestly successful. There are always people trying to subvert democracy for their own ends. They often succeed, as recent events prove even in the stable bulwark of freedom known as the United States. Grassroots movements have made a start in nurturing democracy back to health after the economic crash of 2008. A struggle seems to be impending, and many elites are hoping it will be a violent one. They know how to win those.

16

No More Privacy

"We shall meet in the place where there is no darkness." - *1984*

The Ministry of Love is still, fortunately, not yet reality for most Americans. The technology to institute a Ministry of Love, however, is very much part of the here and now. It is well known that the U.S. government practices torture. Spokesmen for the government deem it "enhanced interrogation." They know they are lying and know we know. They must deny torture because to admit it would necessitate doing something to end it. So they lie about it, no one believes the lie, and until it can be proven (which the government will not allow) the denial holds. The entire adventure is a display of doublethink in its purest form. The same denial works in the case of spying on U.S. citizens without a search warrant. Nobody wants their government spying on them personally, but we are afraid of letting unknown terrorists make their plans freely. So we play the game of denial and doublethink, pretending that our side has only good guys. And a government of good guys would only show its nasty side to bad guys.

Jose Padilla and Bradley Manning are among the tiny number of U.S. born American citizens to have been publicly disappeared on American soil. A third, Edward Snowden, has been disappeared to our old nemesis, Russia. These are not frightening numbers, though it is three more than legally permissible under our Constitution. Padilla is Puerto Rican, converted to Islam, and Manning is gay, so America's cultural and ethnic core retains the appearance of being protected by our laws. Snowden, being Anglo and hetero, is probably more conveniently left far away. Padilla and Manning have been finally brought out for their "speedy and public" trials, but as broken men, having undergone "enhanced interrogations", proving that torture works—not for getting accurate information, but for getting confessions to whatever heinous crimes the government wants, proving the rulers—be they King, Il Duce, Fuhrer, Chairman, Big Brother—are never wrong. These isolated examples from our War on Terror caution everyone to be careful not to attract the attention of the Thought Police. And where can we hide?

Not even hiding in the dark will avail Winston Smith. O'Brien talks to him in his room, while he sleeps. Winston is taken to the Ministry of Love, where the lights are never off. Modern electronic technology proves Big Brother's surveillance resources to be primitive. The scenario is now in place for the corporate state to delve into the secrets of everyone, while its minions effectively hide their misdeeds, even their identities. The Wikileaks scandal, with revelations provided by Manning about government misconduct and incompetence, shows decisively how the elites have rigged the rules to their advantage, and how desperately determined they are to retain this power. The revelations from Wikileaks contain no major surprises, but that is not the issue. To the nation's overlords, turnabout is not fair play, and they will play most foully to instill fear into anyone who would try to make it fair. Whoever might be temporarily in nominal leadership of the country is moot. The secretive, corporate military-industrial complex rules roughshod over leaders and followers alike.

During our most recent Middle Eastern wars, Republican leaders opened the naval base at Guantanamo as a prison where inmates have no rights, and closed it to public view. When the Democrats took power, they tried to close the prison and open it to public view, and could not. The corporate state remains supreme no matter which party wins an election.

Most of us like to see our house on the computer screen, on photos taken from satellites. Some of us remember watching the Sputniks and Vanguards in the late fifties. Safe in the dark, we could watch those tiny lights traverse the night skies. Now they watch us, and GPS trackers and drone technology are on the horizon. Gone is the darkness.

Turning the clock back is impossible, even if we desire to do it. The fact is that the advantages of this electronic age far outweigh the drawbacks. Light, which humanity has always sought, is now available to one and all, to wholly eliminate that terrifying night. All humans everywhere can be reached with the light, and enriched with knowledge. But there are challenges—great opportunities always carry great responsibilities. If privacy in fact is now gone, then we must set new standards for everyone to mind their own business, and hold to these standards zealously. And we must open our governments so our leaders answer to us. This, after all, is what our founding fathers intended, when they brought forth our nation, during the period known historically as the Enlightenment.

17

Empire in the Light

"All of the disputed territories contain valuable minerals, and some of them yield important vegetable products such as rubber....But if they did not exist,the structure of world society, and the process by which it maintains itself, would not be essentially different." - *1984*

In the modern world the concept of public knowledge of all the State's affairs is understandably controversial. After all, we need to hide our plans and schemes from our enemies. Why should we give the bad guys our military and industrial secrets? Theoretically, this is a sound argument, until something like Wikileaks exposes in detail what most of us suspected all along: secrets hide facts that would embarrass government officials far more often than they hide the blueprints for our ultimate weapon. Major advantages in warfare remain in one side's hands for only a short time, no matter how diligently the rulers keep secrets. In times of never-ending war, empire vs. empire, technological advances are generally utilized to serve destructive ends. This reality was obvious to Orwell after WWII. It should be a glaring universal truth now.

Small nations being difficult to govern by the golden rule, it stands to reason an empire must use blood and iron at all times. Leaders of empire must be hard, whether they come to power by treachery, inheritance, or election. Imperial demands will overcome even the most altruistic and high-minded leadership. Small wonder that in modern societies, all of which pay lip service to democratic principles, heard-hearted practices of empire are best kept secret from the commoners. Thus Bradley Manning was accused of treason for giving "aid and comfort to the enemy", which turned out to be the American people.

In his *Outline of History* H.G. Wells titles WWI "The Catastrophe of Modern Imperialism." A century later mankind is more aware than ever of the ugly results of imperial priorities. Woodrow Wilson hoped it would be the "war to end all wars," and it certainly was the war to make mankind wish all wars would end. Worldwide, the human race knows war is too costly to be waged, no matter who wins. Yet we continue to make exceptions. Ancient prejudices still get people swindled, incarcerated, and murdered, which always invites resentment and retaliation. There are always con men willing to exploit these resentments for their own gain. Acting on gut feelings being easier than accepting intellectual concepts, we still have wars. Yet in the brilliant light of electronic media, we can see that our enemies cry as hard as we do when friends and relatives are blown up. What we learned a century ago keeps showing up as reality: war serves no purpose but to reinforce insanity.

In a century our awareness as a race has grown. Still we have wars. Wars are smaller now, useless regarding any social or economic benefit to people. They do accomplish, as Orwell predicted, "destruction, not of human lives, but of the products of human labor." People do not want wars. Still we are fairly easily persuaded to fight them. Empires are hopelessly driven to start what people despise. If war is endemic to empire, it seems that empire has outlived any useful purpose it might once have had.

Empires have always existed so that one ethnic group could exploit others. But historically, only the upper class of the ruling people gained rewards of wealth and privilege. The middle and lower classes of Egypt, Persia, Rome, Spain, Russia, Britain, or America (a most partial list) were charged with conquering subject peoples and keeping them subservient. Socially, the commoners of the imperial rulers could consider themselves superior to the conquered subjects. But cheap goods from conquered provinces reduce the value of everything produced in the homeland. Studies indicate that even in the heralded British Empire, no more than a tenth of the British people were enriched by ruling a quarter of the world. The other nine-tenths suffered financially as a direct result of empire. And the

British Empire was far more egalitarian than most others in history.

When the United Kingdom finally achieved real democracy at the end of WWII, the British people discarded the empire as quickly as they could. Winston Churchill, beloved leader during Britain's fight for its life, lost his post as Prime Minister at war's end, largely because he intended to fight to preserve the Empire. Of course the takeover of imperial duties by the United States (as Orwell noted) facilitated Britain's bailout. But the empire's end would have happened anyway, simply because the majority of Britons realized that having an empire was not worth the trouble of keeping it. And though America and "Airstrip One" have maintained a staunch alliance since, there is no doubt that most British citizens have few regrets about putting down what Kipling heralded as "the White Man's burden."

Since the U.S. took hegemony, living standards for American workers have shrunk despite increased productivity, but the first real loss for American democracy came with the Korean War. An essential piece of the Constitution: the requirement that Congress declare war, went out with a whimper. Since then we have had several wars, not one declared by Congress. So even though we have been at war much of the last sixty years, we have, since the end of WWII, been officially at peace. Congress has over time been way too eager to surrender its duty to the Executive Branch, and the American people have been complicit in this ongoing abdication of responsibility. At the same time we have witnessed a steady erosion of our rights, and mounting public debt and personal privation.

In 2014, many politicians as well as media pundits and average citizens are proposing cuts in Social Security, Medicare, and all other public services in order to pay down debts incurred by ongoing wars. The rich, who reap enormous profits from imperial ventures, are able to easily defeat proposals to raise their taxes, although most American voters believe taxes on wealth should be raised. Some presidents use their war powers more freely than others, yet all presidents retain and jealously guard that imperial prerogative. In addition to war debts (which could conceivably be renounced) we have thousands of

Americans and millions of foreigners killed or maimed, and these numbers are here to stay.

The founding fathers, whom we claim to revere publicly every chance we get, meant to make it hard to get the country into a war. They knew that kings were prone to go to war at the smallest whim, that royal power grew during war-time, and that wars could only enrich the victorious upper class. They wanted elected representatives, answerable directly to the voters, to have the war power. Then, after intense debate, if a majority still perceived justifiable reasons for going to war, we would have it. Under that old-fashioned system the United States since 1789 has declared war on Britain, Mexico, ourselves, Spain, Germany (twice), and Japan. We also had an undeclared war with France, uncounted Indian wars, and military occupations of quite a few countries. If we want war, we can get it.

Now we are told that in the age of rapid transportation and instant communication, the constitutional requirements are too slow. Yet the president, as commander-in-chief, has always had the power to use the military to defend the country. Within a day after Pearl Harbor, the Congress declared war on Japan. What genuine emergency could America possibly face if we rigidly enforced the Law of the Land? Since Korea, the United States has fought several wars, some of them lasting quite long, none of them consequential, at least concerning America's protection. Most of them were proven to be needless adventures based on falsehoods.

We have lived with an imperial presidency for so long we take it for granted. The rationale for Congress's abdication of its war powers has one dubious advantage: we are not responsible for our country's going to war; so much for rule by the people. Yet as was the case with empires of old, we are charged with fighting war, paying for it, and dealing with the dead and wounded. Drones are the latest delusion about war without casualties, but even if this new "ultimate weapon" works the way its promoters say it will, everyone else will soon have it. And we still must pay the bill. The general standard of living will deteriorate further, and we are still in 1984.

There is the premise that we are better off to fight the wrong war than not to fight the right one. Perhaps it is helpful to get this notion into the open, to examine it more clearly for its substance and value. By "right war" we can conclude this to mean necessary war. History shows an overwhelming number of unnecessary wars, from at least one side. A strong argument exists for the allies fighting WWII. But there would have been no WWII if we did not have WWI, which was absolutely unneeded. The only excuse for that conflict is mass insanity, and since then worldwide sanity has taken mankind to the realization that war is good for "absolutely nothing". In this case we can either embrace or reject sanity. To take the sane approach requires conscientious thought and effort. Insanity means more war as peace, ignorance as strength, and freedom as slavery, and we are still in 1984.

No one denies that we live in a rough world, populated by too many mean, vicious, angry fellow travelers. Yet most of us are rational beings, aware that we follow our violent fellows at enormous cost, for no true gain, that the result is more angry people, who encourage one another to more violent acts. We know that people everywhere are about the same, that most people are peaceful, ready to live and let live. In this case allowing warfare to go on is nothing less than mass insanity. Warfare glorifies the sickest personalities among us, and while these people deserve our help, they do not deserve to rule those of us who are relatively sane.

Maintaining an empire lets the sick rule the rest of us.

18

The Party Line

"QUESTION AUTHORITY" - (seen on a bumper sticker)

"One of these days, thought Winston with sudden deep conviction, Syme will be vaporized." - *1984*

"No one who had once fallen into the hands of the Thought Police ever escaped in the end. They were corpses waiting to be sent back to the grave." - *1984*

Anyone with a passing familiarity with working in the corporate world—government, big business, military—is living in 1984. We have all witnessed vaporizations, disappearances, doublethink, and thoughtcrime. Totalitarian despots have taken these concepts to chilling extremes, but they are used by all modern operational enterprises. Party—or company— lines, enforced with varying degrees of rigidity, are ubiquitous in modern human life. Even the remotest hermit exists because he is allowed to by laxness on the part of those in power. "Free people" like ourselves differ from Nazis or Bolsheviks only in degree. Worldwide corporate demands on our lives, liberties and even our thoughts are as much a reality as night, day, or weather. Since the corporate mentality is ubiquitous, we all tend to get used to it. Herein lies its danger, as the powerful can more sternly apply their control, while we scarcely notice the change. By the time we realize we are uncomfortable, we have probably reached a point where it is perilous to challenge authority.

Orwell wrote a scary story. Ingsoc's extremes: everybody watched all the time, with even faint rebellion punished by luring the rebel into a false sense of hope, then yanking him into prison to be tortured and brainwashed until he actually believes with all his heart that his torturers are right, is (and will likely always be) fiction. But good fiction is usually more believable than fact, and the facts are that similarities to Orwell's world abound in our own. In the corporate world people are vaporized all the time—it is called termination or firing. An employee who is fired is never again heard from or talked about. People who do mention a fired employee's name risk disfavour from the bosses, and they never know who among their fellows might tattle. Kiss up and kick down often leads to corporate success.

We look upon firing as much more benign than taking someone from home at night and putting him inside the Ministry of Love. Still, we fear being fired. Most of us must work or undergo privations, and ultimately starvation... innocent spouses and children suffer as well. No one argues with an employer's right not to pay a worker who cannot or will not do his job. But most employers believe that fear alone keeps workers on the job. They fiercely resist any legal measures that would require them to prove an employee is not performing before they can terminate him. The bosses reserve for themselves the right to terminate for any reason or none. They claim that business efficiency requires fear, but right or wrong, they prefer fearful employees.

Civil service rules, unions, and government spending to keep unemployment rates fairly low have tempered workplace fear. But these institutions are under severe and relentless assault in recent years. Big business has led the assault, but many members of the working class have co-operated, not merely out of fear for their personal survival, but from a sincere belief that they are working hard, that others are not, and that they will be recognized and rewarded for their diligence once the dead weight in the workplace has been removed. Working people have turned against their own because they have bought corporate lies.

Whether the unions have failed to state their case credibly, the corporate elites have made their point astoundingly well. All across the country workers vote for politicians who deny workplace rights to "those people", with the result that worker rights are denied to themselves as well. Instead of demanding that employers pay all workers enough to buy back what they produce, they buy the cheapest wares they can find, usually items made in foreign sweatshops, then they wonder why their jobs are vaporized. Worker productivity and profits rise while wages fall, and many in the middle class and the working poor cheer, or at least acquiesce. The one or two percent could not have accomplished such a complete corporate take-over of the society without help from at least some of the other ninety-eight or ninety-nine.

We are steeped in a world of doublethink. We believe only the lazy suffer, that only the smart and hardworking get ahead. Most workers would join unions if they could, yet accept the fact that they cannot as one more "way it is." Most workers are savvy enough not to entertain the illusion that the elites are even remotely concerned with their well-being, yet there is still that strong belief that the invisible hand of the magic market place will bring justice to the world. The myth of the rugged individualist is very much with us, even though corporate business is conducted with corporate power, with no place at all for individualism.

The mainstream media could more thoroughly expose corporate wrongdoing, but media is now a corporate enterprise, so the likelihood of this is improbable. Still, accurate evidence is available from lesser known publications. Those who do not avail themselves of information are compliant in their own exploitation, hence, "Proles and animals are free." With the vast middle class of the twentieth century reduced in financial resources, we are left with a huge majority of working poor, fairly equal in level of poverty. Only those who are aware of this reality can threaten the elites. But we must make use of the information that exists, and act on that information, together. If we ever hear someone like O'Brien in our sleep, promising "We shall meet in the place where there is no darkness," it will be too late.

Part 4 - The Schoolyard Bully

19

Bringing out the Worst

"From the moment when the machine first made its appearance it was clear to all thinking people that the need for human drudgery, and therefore to a great extent for human inequality, had disappeared." - *1984*

Income inequality—also known as obscene wealth—need not exist in the Third Millennium, and would not exist in a democracy. Human ingenuity has made available the resources of life in sufficient quantity to provide all necessities, and even many amenities and some luxuries, to all. Lives of reasonable comfort and security, not only economically but environmentally, could be lived by everyone. Achieving this goal would take planning, which is claimed as taboo in the world of free enterprise. But free enterprise can thrive in a planned economy—and capitalists make plans. The world today has a few living in obscene luxury and huge numbers of fellow human beings living in obscene squalor, because the resources of life are hoarded by those few at the top. Obviously greed implies more than simply having the most money.

If everyone were living comfortable lives, if everyone had meaningful work that provided a good living with some leisure to seek personal goals, being rich would lose its allure. Wealth must enable those who are wealthy to demand and get deference and submission, which are only given when those with the wealth also control the means of living for everyone else. Only scarcity will inspire sufficient fear in the vulgar to make them servile. Under these conditions all classes of humanity endure lives dominated by various types of fear. For this reason every major religion warns against the accumulation of great wealth. The exception is the twisted Calvinism of modern times, as preached by Ayn Rand,

Milton Friedman, and their disciples. Their creed holds that those who accumulate great wealth are fulfilling the natural order of things, and thus deserve every penny they can grab. The prophets of greed (and they do claim that greed is a virtue) believe that when we are all free to get and keep everything we can, individual freedom and material progress will be unrestricted, opening up a new millennium of prosperity for us all.

As nice as the promise sounds, history tells us a different story, that economic inequality leads to mass poverty, despotism, war, and misery. Many of the preachers of unmitigated greed know better, but they also know that submission to the rich by fooling the hayseeds pays better than hard work. The wealthy can only receive the subservience they demand by making everyone else desperate to get some of that wealth. The situation only exists when the illusion is widely accepted that those who have all the money are entitled to it. So they pay well anyone who can use words to promote the illusion.

The reward of greed, then, is power, as the reward of alcohol is drunkenness. And just as some people can drink liquor without becoming sots, some can accrue huge fortunes without being consumed by greed. These are the wealthy people, such as Buffet, Gates, and Soros, who believe that money needs to be redistributed to keep the society functioning. Wealth, in their case, has not interfered with common sense. But those who succumb to the sense of power that comes from wealth have abandoned common sense. Like any addict, they will sacrifice anything to retain that power. And of course, as it is with any addiction, power, no matter how absolute, is never enough. The phrase "drunk on power" tells the human race's sad story over and over.

Orwell's Inner Party members have distilled the addiction to power down to its purest form. Living only slightly more comfortable lives than those in the Outer Party and the Proletariat, they nonetheless control the productive capacity of society. By depriving everyone else, they are able to control people with a totality historical dictators could only dream of. Stalin had very few personal possessions he could call his own, but in reality he owned nine million square miles of empire, and everything in it.

As a result, he owned everybody, too.

Obviously Stalin was a bully. But O'Brien derides Stalin for holding the delusion that he bullied people for the betterment of the human race. O'Brien, and the others in the Inner Party are under no such delusion. For them, "God is Power," and with true belief in that creed, they are able to push people around, beat them, starve them, hurt them, and in the end make their victims believe they really are superior. Orwell reduces the despotic mentality to that of the teenaged schoolyard bully.

And like the bully of adolescence, he can befriend Winston, make him feel secure, then suddenly turn on him, have his flunkies beat him mercilessly, until there is nothing left inside the shell that used to be Winston Smith. O'Brien not only makes Winston say "Uncle." He makes him mean it. The logical conclusion of unfettered economic inequality leads to rule by a coterie of adolescent psychopaths. With the adults gone from the schoolyard, the meanest kids are in charge.

20

The Envy of Us All

"Without a middle class, any democracy is doomed." - Thom Hartmann, *Screwed: The Undeclared War on the Middle Class*

While greed might be on some peoples' list of virtues now, envy is still one of the deadly sins, as the spokespeople for the wealthy never hesitate to point out whenever anyone publicly suggests the elites ought to pay higher taxes, obey laws to protect consumers, workers, or the environment, or otherwise aid the progress of the human race. The Ministry of Truth cranks out the party line: great wealth is the product of hard work and high intelligence, and every wealthy person is entitled to every nickel he can get. If rich people want to share, that is of course their right. But according to the Rand/Friedman cult, there is no moral right for government to force the rich to share. By this creed, anyone who proposes such confiscatory outrages is guilty of class envy.

No one wants to be envious, to practice one of mankind's most distasteful emotions. Mature adults prefer to count their blessings rather than covet what others have. But the mere fact that we are accused of envy is no confirmation that we are guilty of it. If we buy into this accusation, we are submitting to the bullies once again...if we envy them, we are admitting their superiority.

In fact, raising taxes on the wealthy during recessions is far more pragmatic than simply doing nothing, waiting and hoping for happy days to come back. Throughout our history we have proven over and again that when a few people accumulate massive wealth, the rest of us undergo hardships. Spokespeople for the elites, who usually celebrate the amorality of the marketplace, suddenly claim moral shock that people would want to confiscate money from those who have it. When their entitlements are challenged by the immorality of people starving while the few hoard obscene wealth, they are quick to remind us the world has no morals. Like bullies everywhere, the elites conveniently claim both sides of the issue.

If, as the elites claim, the problem with socialism is that eventually you run out of somebody else's money, the problem with capitalism is that eventually only a tiny few have all the money. Both adages claim the moral high ground. Scruples aside, we must decide on the method that allows for the greatest good for the most people.

Liberals and progressives do not seriously argue for total economic equality. There are no Bolsheviks left, at least in any circles where they might have influence. Liberal policies are in many ways moderate or conservative, in the traditional definitions. Social Security and Medicare are the status quo. Conservatives like things as they are. Proposals to eliminate these extremely popular government programs are actually radical. These programs keep many old people from falling into chill penury, but they make no approach toward economic equality.

To call people who defend them socialist is laughably unrealistic. Yet the apologists for hoarded wealth keep repeating the Big Lie.

Another Big Lie tells us that if the elites can keep all their money they will invest it in job-creating businesses, which will lead to widespread prosperity. Anyone who follows true history knows better. We know hard times are caused by reduced consumer spending. When people buy less, employers reduce their payrolls. Higher unemployment means less spending. The vicious cycle is broken when government stimulates the economy by creating jobs. The alternative—to do nothing and let the economy hit bottom and start working its way up again-causes much misery. People tend to act unpredictably under circumstances of prolonged misery. Government spending on public works projects has often saved capitalism from itself.

Government spending does not impoverish the well-to-do. Neither do progressive taxes. But by easing the hardships of recession (and in some cases avoiding recession) they do lessen economic inequality. When people are not desperately impoverished, (or constantly worried about becoming impoverished) they tend to have more self-respect, to be less deferent toward those who possess money. In short, people who are economically secure are not so easily bullied. Proposals to spend money on public works projects, proposals to raise taxes on those who still possess wealth when many are poor, can be debated and discussed on practical merits. Democracies thrive when more people contribute opinions on solving problems. But to reject these practical solutions outright, to brand any effort to lessen economic inequality as "socialist class warfare" in an effort to end debate before it starts, is another matter. It indicates that merely having money is not what the elites want. It suggests that they are addicted to the power that goes with money, and they will take harsh and desperate measures to keep it. The elites want us to envy them…it indicates that we believe in their superiority. "God is Power."

21

The Survival of the Race

"You are under the impression that hatred is more exhausting than love. Why should it be? And if it were, what difference would it make? Suppose that we choose to wear it out faster. Suppose that we quicken the tempo of human life till men are senile at thirty. Still, what difference would it make?" - *1984*

Obviously, bullies, whether in the schoolyard, the boardroom, or any other situation, are uninterested in the future. They seek only to assuage whatever demons they are haunted by, by demonizing others. To ease the pain they feel, they hurt others. To alleviate their fears, they frighten others. To point out to them the possibility of a bright future based on cooperation would be useless. Most bullies do grow up, as they find there are people and organizations far tougher, crueller, and craftier than they are. They change their behaviour to the point where they avoid causing damages that can get them into trouble. Or they adjust to living out troubled existences, usually surrounded by people of similar psychopathic tendencies. But some, due to combinations of circumstances, are able to bully throughout their lives, eliminating competitors to the point where they are in charge of vast enterprises, or countries. A sensible goal of rational people everywhere would be to combine our minds, hearts and actions to prevent such results as much as we possibly can.

The *U.S. Constitution* was enacted to enable people to work together to keep bullies from taking power. For over two centuries it has allowed people to form substantial opposition to absolute bullying. Over time, plutocrats have found ways to circumvent the law of the land, or to twist it to serve their selfish ends, in total disregard for the prospects of humanity. At the outset of the Third Millennium, we find ourselves living with social and economic inequalities unseen in our history since before the Great Depression. Voters in recent elections have been forced to choose between brutal inequality and inequality of a more benign nature. Regardless of who wins the elections, the Upper classes in the Land of the Free are in control, and have the means to remain so. Most commoners have cynically accepted this status as the natural order of things.

The economic disaster that began in 2008 still wreaks havoc on the Middle class, reducing most of its members to the level of working poor. Privation and uncertainty have eliminated the Middle as any threat to the power of the Upper, but the middle class and the working poor are now effectively one class. Working together they could restore honest economic, social and political democracy. Obviously the elites intend to prevent our enlightenment. Since the Supreme Court with the "Citizens' United" ruling allowed corporations to spend as much money as they want to influence elections, the Uppers can now overwhelm any opposing points of view, buy politicians who will do their bidding, and convince the rest of us that resistance is futile. They can afford it.

In an atmosphere of condoned hopelessness, it is tempting to give in, to make the best of the despair that is the human condition, to ignore as much as possible the dismal reality. By abdicating our responsibilities for our own liberty, we achieve a different freedom: "Proles and animals are free."

22

Push Back Or Suck It Up

"Perhaps the forces that now menace freedom are too strong to be resisted for very long. It is still our duty to do whatever we can to resist them." - Aldous Huxley, *Brave New World Revisited*

"Two gin-scented tears trickled down the sides of his nose. But it was all right, everything was all right, the struggle was finished. He had won the victory over himself. He loved Big Brother. THE END - *1984*

The plutocrats and their defenders present us with two choices: one is to accept and enhance their greed; the other is to admit to envy, and thence try to cure our insanity by learning how to accept and enhance their greed. The rules of the game are rigged, and we are left with O'Brien's view of the future: "a boot stomping on a human face—forever." The stomping need not include the physical act, though we know the machinery is here for doing so, if the elites ever deem it necessary. For now, however, the science of mind control has improved considerably since Orwell's time, and Madison Avenue is far more effective than the Ministry of Truth. The Supreme Court, by allowing unlimited corporate spending in political campaigns, has given the upper class the go-ahead to spend all it needs to drown out all opposition in all media. As it happened, in 2012 the propaganda machine was not well funded enough. We can expect the next election cycle to witness an enormous increase in spending on the part of the plutocrats. The Big Lie will be told.

The scale is astounding. A prole who gives ten dollars to a political campaign suffers more financially than someone of the one percent who gives a million. Satisfaction for the small donor is limited to helping someone he likes win elections. If his candidate wins, he may see legislation enacted that will improve conditions for his class. The plutocrat gets full-service politicians for his money. Resources, tax hedges, labour laws, and regulations will be geared to the rich man's desires. He will get his investment back manifold. And more money buys more power.

Next time that ten-dollar campaign contribution will hurt the worker even more. The middle class got mauled in the Great Recession. The working poor have suffered the same fate. It might be beneficial for people in both groups to work together to restore economic, social, and political democracy. If this suggestion sounds Marxist, it is nonetheless reality based. The middle and lower classes have more in common than they have apart, and in 2013 our commonality is more apparent than it has been in a long time. It remains to be seen whether the Proles will awake (our source of hope). Now nearly half of the eligible voters (overwhelmingly of the middle class and working poor) cannot be bothered with voting every two years, and the plutocrats are still firmly in charge. The corporate propaganda machine still convinces many that we are free, while the corporate state relentlessly locks up power.

What of the present day Winston Smiths? There are many of us, and we are not limited to hazy memories and a small newspaper clipping to show us that reality is different from the official picture we are shown. We can reason better than Winston could. Though critical thinking is not an educational priority in the Third Millennium, it is not yet totally renounced. Perhaps Winston really was the "last man"—the last, sickly remnant of a race that could put facts together, make conclusions from facts, and form reasonable arguments to challenge the propaganda delivered from the top. But deprived of food, water, air, shelter, and contact with others having similar capabilities, suffering physical and mental abuse, he is a wretched survivor, in no way fit to stand against a murderous despotism with insatiable lust for power. We have access to reality, and the resources to share it, despite the volume of disinformation spewing from our Ministry of Truth. Our brotherhood is seven billion strong. We need only exert ourselves to make the connections. We are obliged to make the effort, because our inertia now truly will stunt and starve some future "last man."

O'Brien tells Winston he is insane, and from a standpoint of self- preservation, this is true. How many times have we been tempted to speak truth to power, only to refrain because we know that power does not appreciate truth? We know well that the consequences of speaking out in a corporate setting, ranging from inconvenient disapproval to mortal privation, are too severe for a sane person to risk. We tend to cluck with disapproval at the crazy people who do speak out. Popular wisdom holds that we get along only if we go along. Usually the results of practicing this philosophy are harmless, ending in small bits of self-disappointment countered by knowledge of discretion as the better part of valour. But there are times when some of us are left with the insane decision to risk jail by refusing to be drafted, in opposition to the supposedly "sane" choice of going to war. Inmates of Stalin's Gulag were routinely judged insane, and in light of what happened to them when they committed their crimes against the State, they were. So it is in Winston's case.

Winston knows he has gone too far by starting his diary. Simply thinking about it is the crime: Thoughtcrime. He knows that whether he writes his diary or not, sooner later he will give himself away and he will be guilty of thought, the only crime there is. To be accused by the Thought Police is to be guilty. The Nazis and the Bolsheviks, among others, proved again and again that torture works when the goal is a confession to whatever atrocities the State accuses someone of committing. Torture proves every time that Big Brother (or Uncle Joe or The Fuhrer) is infallible. And the government of the United States, promoting "enhanced interrogation" knows that.

Cruelty, like kindness, is integral to the human condition. But since the dawn of complex society, around the end of the Neolithic Age, people in power have been aware of the power of pain to coerce people into obedience. By the twentieth century, with the help of science, authorities learned how to prolong life while defeating hope and breaking defiance. New levels of power could be reached, so new goals of power were set. Techniques of coercion through pain have improved immeasurably in the ensuing century. Dictators have become adept at making their subjects cry "Uncle."

Envy gives part of the envious one's spirit to the envied one, without asking. Politicians and pundits who preach the cause of the wealthy make the accusation of "class envy" to remind everyone that the wealthy are in a superior position because they are indeed superior. Therefore, we commoners are advised to emulate the rich rather than try to take what rightfully belongs to them, no matter how badly we need it. As for helping the poor, the longstanding belief in our culture is that the poor have only themselves to blame. If they would only do as the rich do (bribe politicians, for instance) they too would grow rich. Accusations of envy are tricks of sophisticated bullies. The purpose is to forestall rational debate about public policies such as tax laws, so those who have can keep it without having to spread it around, which would allow others to prosper also. Stopping debate before it begins means the common folk will continue to show the proper sycophantic respect to the uppers. Bullies need that.

23

Many Mansions in the Ministry of Love

"The citizen of Oceania is not allowed to know anything of the tenets of the other two philosophies, but he is taught to execrate them as barbarous outrages upon morality and common sense. Actually the three philosophies are barely distinguishable, and the social systems they support are not distinguishable at all." - *1984*

As a serious writer Orwell pointed out the direction the world seemed to be heading just after WWII. The three super-states do exist, though other nations or alliances can challenge the absolute power of the big three. This difference is not readily noticeable, however, to the child whose soldier father never came home, to the goatherd who will never leave Guantanamo, to the private who goes slowly insane in a military brig while awaiting his constitutionally guaranteed "speedy and public trial." Examples are limitless. The rest of us are left alone, free as proles. We are even allowed to criticize the corporate state…for the nonce.

Although torture is illegal by U.S. law and international treaties we have signed, everyone knows our government tortures. Many in official circles, as well as in the punditry and general public, reserve the right to do so, as long as we do it to "those people." This concept is chillingly reminiscent of Orwell's world. Supporters of enhanced interrogation in the government and media know well that torture can get—not truth, but confessions as desired by the interrogators. Despite the fact that most Americans disapprove of torture, we are unable to get a vote on it, and we still have the mechanisms, regardless of who has won the last election. In this respect our society is even with 1984.

The difference in important matters between "us" and "them" is virtually non-existent. If anyone can be vaporized and tortured, all of us can. No cause is so righteous that it seems justifiable to anyone being tortured in its behalf... unless that person can be tortured endlessly, until he is completely remade in the torturers' image. In most cases attention to that sort of detail is unnecessary. In a way it was quite thoughtful of O'Brien to take so much time and trouble to cure Winston's "insanity." Mere compliance is what the modern corporate state wants, and the knowledge that people can be disappeared, kept in isolation without limits, and ultimately broken, is sufficient to keep the general population cowed. In Orwell's world the pretext for authoritarian rule is "the People." In our world it is "free enterprise" and "rugged individualism." To those under the boot, or to those who are cowed into compliance by fear of the boot, the philosophy is not worth consideration.

In the last part of the Twentieth Century, rulers have learnt that populations can be controlled without the unreasoning, fanatical brutality used by the Bolsheviks, Nazis, and Ingsoc Party, among others. Modern dictators maintain power while imprisoning and torturing only a fraction of those who were vaporized by earlier regimes. Surgical knives are less costly than chainsaws, and just as effective, with the added double- think illusion that only the guilty are being punished. Proles and animals being free, the modern corporate state has simply increased the population of proles. Only the people in the "Middle," who feel something is amiss and believe they can do something about it, are considered a threat. The vast number of the enlarged proletariat (which includes the working poor, small businessmen, the growing pool of unemployed and newly impoverished middle class) will be left alone as long as they feel their condition is hopeless, and persevere at doing nothing about it.

The U.S. government can imprison anyone indefinitely, for any reason or none. Any statute granting it such power (few do, which is only a small deterrent to the government's abuse of power) goes against the Bill of Rights. It is understood that no right is absolute, that they all entail responsibilities, that society can and should regulate our actions so that no one's rights can intrude on the rights of others. But it is also understood that the founders intended for exceptions to be fully debated in the open, and that once enacted, these exceptions would always be subject to further debate. In contrast, police state measures carried out by the United States of America are seldom discussed until they are discovered, temporarily embarrassing whatever elected government appears to be nominally in charge. Government will fight hard to retain its powers. Even when its conduct is deemed illegal by the courts, the bureaucracy of the Executive branch has ways to delay or defy the rulings of the courts. And we are well aware of a growing willingness of the courts to take the government's part.

Authoritarian measures are justified by government spokespeople, news commentators, and citizens as necessary to preserve our safety in a world full of enemies. This argument is understandably troubling to those of us who would preserve the Bill of Rights. Safety is an issue of vast connotations, yet traffic lights are not in the same category as secret prisons. Restricting our rights that we could be kept safe ought to be debated in the open, but secret government operatives seem to prefer to act in the dark, which they are allowed to do more freely in times of fear than times of peace. Whether or not the corporate State is consciously working to keep the public fearful, we are hard put to deny that the perceived foreign threats keep coming. A few more crises, a few more shocks, and we could find ourselves living in a despotic world where there no laws and only one crime.

24

Fascists Among Us

"From the 1970's, changes in the international economy have put new weapons in the hands of the masters, enabling them to chip away at the hated social contract that had been won by popular struggle." - Noam Chomsky, *Profit Over People*

"The Will to Order can make tyrants out of those who merely aspire to clean up a mess." - Aldous Huxley, *Brave New World Revisited*

The concept of thoughtcrime has two interdependent facets. The primary part is that anyone who thinks Big Brother is wrong in even the tiniest way is guilty of a crime. The corollary is that if someone in authority thinks, or says, a person has committed thoughtcrime, that person is instantly guilty. In either case he will be vaporized, tortured, brainwashed and ultimately executed. In any society where the single capital crime is thought, people, being capable of thought, are all guilty, and the implementation of punishment is only a matter of time. Without doubt, sooner or later even O'Brien was heard uttering "Down with Big Brother" in his sleep.

While the concept of thoughtcrime is, when held up to the light, ridiculous, we cannot forget that many people would like to control the opinions (as well as the actions) of everyone else, and that some of those have such a hatred for the human race that they sincerely believe that all, being able to think, ought to be condemned. The fact that we are at this time able to argue against the policies of a secretive, military-corporate state is no cause for complacency. The time to act is when the danger is not yet upon us, when we still have access to information and the right to share that information and to collectively react. Although the State has the preponderant possession of information and a well-financed and highly efficient means of altering that information to serve its ends, the reality is still available to those who want it. But soft power is power nonetheless, and we dare not be content to allow the rulers to retain it. Soft power can become brutally hard quickly, and when and how will not be matters of debate.

Brute force is available when the establishment wants to use it. During the Occupy protests of 2011, police state methods were widely used, and while probably most Americans abhorred it, many of our countrymen applauded. For government to convince even a minority of Americans to approve such direct and brutal violations of the Bill of Rights, that government has to convince many people that our land and way of life are facing threats so horrid that we must violate our dearest values. And yet, historically, governments at all levels have for the most part been able to suppress dissent violently, with relatively small consequences. Police state methods are used because a large part of our population likes them—again, as long as they are used against "those people."

When brutality, injustice, and economic inequality begin to affect large numbers, when "those people" become "us" there is an opportunity to raise the awareness of the greater society to the threat against us all. The elites, dependent on ignorance, (our ignorance being their strength) stand to lose control when the commoners realize they are all being dominated, albeit some undergo more painful domination than do others.

The Southern United States were de facto dictatorships for many years because poor Whites were routinely taught to fear the Blacks with whom they had much more in common than apart. The KKK served as the aristocrats' secret police. The dictatorship was also operational in other parts of the country, although not as absolutely as in the South. Protests in the fifties and sixties against Jim Crow laws were successful because for a time, a vocal and active number of white Americans became aware that the dictatorship in modern times could not be contained in the South.

Protests for racial equality went hand-in-hand with growing awareness of social inequality everywhere. At the same time public opinion was growing against war in Vietnam. Working together, these movements strengthened each other. The establishment was challenged, lost two presidents, had to negate a colonial war in Vietnam, and was in real danger of seeing its political domination unravel, as a result of a mostly peaceful revolution. The revolution was an alliance of the middle class with the working poor, and some elites (those who were not enslaved by their wealth). The military-industrial complex, on which the rulers depended to maintain power, became a laughing stock. Politicians, business leaders, and media idols were similarly satirized. An era of the four freedoms: freedom of speech and religion, freedom from want and fear, seemed to be, if not within reach, at least plausible.

The establishment regrouped. Many proles feared all the changes, and the elites efficiently exploited their desire for a return to less chaotic times, to retake power. The counter-offensive was signaled by a few assassinations and large-scale violence against dissent. At the virtual apex of the revolution's success, Richard Daly sent the

Chicago police in to suppress protesters during the Democratic nominating convention. The suppression was violent, and overall it was cheered by mainstream America. Those cheers were used by the elites to drive their way back into control. By the early eighties, there was no hint left of the revolutionary spirit.

In addition to Vietnam and the push for racial equality, there were several other shocks to American comfort and complacency: Watergate, Richard Nixon's resignation, Russia's invasion of Afghanistan, the energy crisis, Japan's economic ascendancy, revolts against U.S. puppets in Latin America, the Iranian hostage crisis. Americans began to seek security, which the elites promised, if we would but return them to their cherished place of authority, which they had had back when all was well. Under cover of praise for "freedom" and "rugged individualism" the corporate State managed to regain control. Small wars kept the masses happy while consuming surplus produc-tion and covering up the workings of big business and the military-industrial complex to seal their power. War, which had been a duty of the citi-zenry, would be carried out from then on by a small professional class, who would fight in small wars, easily won, so the public would remain enthusiastic about fighting them. Whether consciously or not, the elites were using *1984* as an instruction manual.

The power structure was supported, in election after election, by majorities of middle class voters, and many in the working poor. The national dialogue was all about restoring our country's greatness, which apparently meant making Americans feel good about themselves by winning a series of small wars against small countries, while concurrently allowing big business to keep more and more of what the country produced. The two major parties (after a period of soul searching by some members of both) were back in thrall to the power elite, different only in detail. People voted for the lesser of two evils, and anyone who chose to vote for actual change knew his or her vote would be thrown away. Wars went on, and the State accrued more power over individuals while it abdicated responsibility toward the citizens. Average Americans wryly boasted their toughness while determinedly changing nothing.

Fascism by other names had established itself, and many Americans seemed to relish the security it promised.

25

Threats to Perpetual Power

"There are only four ways in which a ruling group can fall from power. Either it is conquered from without, or it governs so inefficiently that the masses are stirred to revolt, or it allows a strong and discontented Middle Group to come into being, or it loses its own self-confidence and willingness to govern." - *1984*

"What de Toqueville says of a tyrannical government is true of all totalitarian orders—their moment of greatest danger is when they begin to reform, that is to say, when they begin to show liberal tendencies." - Eric Hoffer, *The True Believer*

With the possibility of foreign conquest eliminated, the American ruling class, having reduced the middle class to near penury, is obviously confident. Change can only happen when people recognize the many serious economic, social, and environmental problems mankind is facing. Politicians serving the ruling elites seem determined not to recognize our difficulties, much less do anything about them. A stalemated national government squabbles while bridges collapse, psychotics with guns and bombs wreak terror, victims of natural disasters languish without help—the list extends. Wealth and power have increased manifold for the upper class over the past forty years, and now their minions ignore the public's oft-stated priorities while they boldly gerrymander electoral districts and restrict poor citizens from voting. The "Citizens' United" gift from the Supreme Court to the corporate world keeps on giving. The Uppers have every reason to be confident.

Still, there is opportunity here, if people recognize and act upon their common economic, social, and environmental needs. The ineptness of the rulers presents a chance, if we take it, to work together to install a government of, by, and for the people. That this idea sounds so corny should tell us how hopelessly cynical our general attitude has grown. But if calling for collective solutions to our common problems seems somehow naïve, we must remember that the problems we now face threaten civilization itself, and that the current political establishment, at the federal, state, and local levels, is either unable or unwilling to do anything to solve them. Corporate power received a setback in 2012, because many Americans—even some proles—became aware and alarmed at the growing income inequality and the erosion of freedom, endless warfare and environmental deterioration, and voted their self-interest despite widespread barriers to exercising their franchise. But the elites are regrouping, as they always do, and are steadfastly reestablishing their power.

If the elites have not been waging war against the middle class, they have been consistently lucky since the early 1980's. Their political servants chipped away at the gains the commoners had made since the Great Depression. Resulting economic inequality brought us inevitably to a Great Recession. In the thirties the middle class and the proletarians, lumped into a single, massive, impoverished class, acted together to change the rules of governance so that life could improve for the common people. Collective actions worked to restore social and economic democracy, resulting in a long period of relative prosperity for all. The causes of the Recession being the same as those of the Depression, it stands to reason that the solutions are the same: raising taxes on the few who still have plenty of money to get money circulating again; government borrowing to further increase circulation; projects to rebuild the infrastructure and improve the environment which will employ workers, who will start buying things, which will restore the private economy to health. These solutions work, yet we are forced to fire government employees, endure deteriorating infrastructure and environment, and live with growing poverty in what is still a land of plenty.

People seem powerless to prevent the deterioration. Still, there is an opportunity to make changes for the better, if we choose to accept it.

We can build united efforts by all citizens who do not own and control the means of production and distribution to restore overall prosperity. Solutions of this type are routinely derided as "socialist", with connotations of Stalin and Mao. Any idea that can be labeled as such is immediately discounted in public debate. Smart people abound who are paid well to pitch the cause of the elites. While Ingsoc is a parody of communism, modern fascism in the West has no problem with individual enrichment, provided the wealth remains in the upper class. The trappings may change from despot to despot, but God still is Power.

Madison Avenue is far more effective at opinion manipulation than the Ministry of Truth could ever hope to be. The modern corporate State pledges fealty to concepts like "rugged individualism" and "free enterprise." What the State actually represents is an intolerant, top-down despotism in which everyone is expected to follow the company line without question, in which the corporation squashes all competition, in which the few at the top keep the profits for themselves. In contrast Stalin, who legally owned only a few personal items, in truth owned the Soviet Empire. His most loyal party apparatchiks also made nice profits on the Black Market, since they had exclusive access to resources. Of course, they always risked vaporization should they ever fall out of Uncle Joe's loving sway. And unlike Big Brother, Uncle Joe died.

The demise of Stalin ultimately led to the unraveling of the Soviet Empire, though Russia remains an invulnerable super-state. Since the implosion of the Soviet Union, the outer party apparatchiks who took over have relentlessly sought to solidify their power, forming a new corporate plutocracy. Unable to correct the inefficiency of Stalin's reign of terror, his inner party successors lost confidence, and were eventually deposed by a powerful middle group. American elites are determined to avoid the same fate—not out of a sense of identification with the communist commissars, but more fundamentally, because they must be obeyed. With information about the failures of past oligarchies readily available, it stands to reason that our ruling elites, like the Inner Party members of Ingsoc, study history.

Once O'Brien gets Winston under his domination in the deeps of the Ministry of Love, he arrogantly reveals the secret: the Party is not interested in governing, but only in ruling, absolutely and always. The famous dictators of the twentieth century had the same lust. However, they found out that being in power required them to pay at least minimal attention to the banal activities needed to assure the functioning of society—what we regard as governing. The Nazis and Fascists started a war to hide their incompetence. But it became too big a war and they were replaced by foreign conquest. The Bolsheviks avoided that fate, but as wars became too dangerous they could not keep the population fearful enough of foreigners to assure continued blind obedience. Communist inefficiency became obvious to all, and the population, led by an organized and angry Middle group, deposed them, much to the surprise of the world at large.

O'Brien never disguised his contempt for past dictators, which is probably typical of anyone currently in power anywhere. Still, with propaganda always blaring to a captive audience how successful the Party is at governing, the Party at some point must make good on some of that hype. Here is the problem rulers have always faced: to convince people that the Uppers are competent governors, without actually governing. Governing requires patience, compromise, tolerance, and hard, boring work—qualities to be found in short supply among the power-mad, among bullies. It also requires financial investment, which plutocrats are loath to make. History tells of a few enlightened monarchs and benevolent dictators whose policies improved the lot of their subjects. And Hitler built the Autobahn, while Mussolini made the trains run on time. But exceptions such as these have become increasingly difficult among modern autocrats. To hold power now is to compulsively and consistently reject public works. O'Brien knows this, which explains why the quality of life in Oceania is at all levels poor.

The downfall of the Soviet State demonstrates the dilemma of ruling when the rulers are obliged to govern. Compromise, tolerance and patience open the way for more of the same, as people begin to see the benefits of self-government, which of course lessens absolute power. Stalin's reign of terror had rendered the people so miserable that their desperation could overcome their fear. As a result, his heirs had no choice but to try to govern. Slight lessening of control made few significant improvements, but it did give people a desire to be heard. From that point the rigidity of the Bolshevik state became a handicap to the elite. Yet they could not democratize the communist system without losing their own power. They needed to govern, and they could not.

The end of Bolshevism did not improve the living standard for most Russians. Russia's new rulers are dedicated to the gospel of greed, as are the elites in the United States, and Mao's heirs in China. This proves Orwell's point: that changing rulers alone will not help the commoners. We can only improve our lot if we accept our commonality, and demand social and economic democracy, without which political democracy cannot work. The destitution of the middle class in our time opens opportunities for the Middles and the Lowers to work together. Under similar circumstances in the thirties, the middle class and the proles promoted their common interests, resulting in general prosperity

and growing democracy for the next two genera-
tions. In the early years of the Third Millennium,
elites worldwide are cooperating to tighten their
control. Despite occasional setbacks, they will
never give up their quest for absolute power.

And they learn from the past.

26

To the Rescue: Guns!

"Show me a bully, and I'll show you someone who is being bullied." (From an anti-bullying program, California public schools, 2008-10)

Among America's epidemic of mass shootings, one, occuring on January 10, 2013, in Taft, California, is exceptional. The assailant used a shotgun instead of an assault rifle (which reduced the casualties to three injuries) and he was captured alive. Since he is in custody, we have a chance to learn why he did what he did, which could give us important clues as to why others do it. He claimed one of the schoolmates he shot was bullying him, to which a witness attested. Concern over bullying is now added to the growing worry about the amount and frequency of gun violence in America. Since bullying is the bedrock of a police state, we might glean some ideas about rolling back the relentless advance of authoritarian rule in our society. At least, we might see what will not work.

From the Taft incident, we conclude that people who are bullied get scared. Actions based on fear tend to be ill-advised, unhealthy. The child who made the assault got one set of bullies off his back, but he is now in the hands of law enforcement, which depends at least somewhat on bullying to function. He will be tried as an adult and sent to prison, where bullying is guaranteed. Perhaps violence against bullying is unhelpful. If an individual shooting rampage fails to alleviate bullying, the argument for guns as an antidote to a bullying dictatorship is open to serious questioning.

Most Americans, whether or not they own guns, ardently want to reduce the horrible toll of gun violence. Reasonable controls on gun distribution and ownership, like reasonable controls on all human activities, could help. Like every right we have, the right to keep and bear arms is not absolute. But fear generally trumps reason, at least initially, and in the case of gun rights, the fear of an emerging police state tempts many citizens to rely on a heavily armed citizenry as a last resort against despots. Thus, the argument goes, all weapons, no matter how destructive, should always be available to everyone. The possibility of psychotics' getting the most sophisticated and deadly weaponry is, to the gun advocates, worth the risk.

Tyrants, to the true believers of the gun movement, are only responsive to violence against them. In support of their belief they point to the American Revolution. While it is true that violence on the part of American rebels helped liberate the thirteen colonies, there are other factors involved (such as alliances with the French, Spanish, and Dutch empires, the incredible distance between America and the British Isles, and the lukewarm attitude of many Britons toward violence against their own) which are of no importance to the firearm fanatics. As the saying goes: "If not for guns, we'd still be British." We might as well say, "If not for guns, we'd all have health care." From the observation that the use of firearms prodded George III into setting his colonies free, they reach the conclusion that a citizenry fully armed with modern weapons is the only hope we have of avoiding or defeating any future American tyrants. And the incessant gun violence in our culture is in their view a price worth paying.

So proponenets of widespread availability of guns are ready to make revolution when the time comes. They are vague concerning the details of the coming tyranny. They will know, it seems instinctively, when the predicted despotism will be upon us. They will act as one to kill the despots' helpers and restore our freedom. Until then, liberals' fears of corporate takeover of the government, the military-industrial complex, economic and social inequality, and endless war —in short anything in this book—are nothing to worry about. The true believers among the gun owners, represented (or manipulated) by the National Rifle Association, would have us depend on them, with their sophisticated weapons, to preserve our rights.

Where were the gun enthusiasts during the Occupy Wall Street protests? Imagine the headline photos, showing squads of heavily-armed NRA members, warning the police to leave the non-violent protesters alone. But the police pepper-sprayed the protesters with no interference from the gun lobby. Going further, the politicians who are most vocal in their support of complete freedom for gun owners, who receive the most generous support from the NRA, tend to be the same ones who are the most enthusiastic in their support of the corporate state, which is as we know, the quintessence of fascism. And NRA members tend to vote single-mindedly the same way.

It is understood that not all gun owners vote with the NRA, that most of them vote their individual interests as they perceive them at election time. We cannot look into peoples' minds and know their motives (though we know there are agents within government bureaucracies working on that). What we can do is look at general trends, and conclude that the most stubborn advocates of the right of everyone to own all types of advanced weaponry, also vote for politicians who unquestioningly serve the corporate state. Whether they know it or not, the true believers of the Second Amendment support politicians who strive to restrict the other nine points of the Bill of Rights.

During this wait—a day, a year, a century—for the coming American dictatorship, all people, including criminals and the seriously deranged, are allowed have access to modern weapons. The argument of the gun lobby is that all citizens should get the same weapons the police and military have. Criminal justice in a functioning society requires that the police have superior weaponry to criminals. A fair fight between the crooks and cops renders protection of the law-abiding citizens virtually impossible. Of course, to the gun lobby, that problem could be solved if all of us simply went about fully armed and ready all the time. The gun lobby's creed, that their weapons are the sole guarantor of our liberty, wears thin when we are presented with the bloodshed, chaos and misery that is certain to continue if we retain the status quo in which anybody can easily get advanced killing machines.

Firearms, within reason, are among the rights we have as free people. Nobody seriously proposes that people who distrust the police (for many substantial reasons) should not have guns to protect their lives, families and property. But an armed insurrection against an imaginary tyrant is not going to happen, nor should it. The founders took seriously the enlightenment principle that free men can work peacefully for the betterment of all. They wrote into the Law of the Land a system of government designed to promote the general welfare without the use of arms. We have had peaceful revolutions under this system. We can have more. But the system only works when most of us use it. We are obliged to keep the bullies at bay with daily practice of the freedoms we have. In a society where our differences are settled with gunfire, the biggest bullies will win.

And should there be an armed rebellion, the Thought Police will simply send out drones.

27

It's Not That Bad?

"Freedom is never voluntarily given by the oppressors. It must be demanded by the oppressed." - Dr. Martin Luther King, Jr.

"Liberty is about our rights to question everything." - Ai Weiwei, Chinese activist

King was feared by the elites not only because he alerted many proles to their situation. He convinced them they need not tolerate it. He was killed over the issue, and many freedom-loving Americans thought he deserved it. We have not reached the point in the Orwellian drama where he would have been vaporized long before he could make any trouble, but many in our society are convinced he was a trouble-maker. Because King was black and most of the people who despise him are white, we obviously have a way to go before we reach that point described in 1984 where all men are equal under the boot, where Inca party members dominate Peru while Englishmen (and at least one psychotic Irishman) rule "Airstrip One." This is a cosmetic point, however, as fascism will manipulate any racial, ethnic, or religious prejudice it finds useful. The Nazis proved this most horribly, and judging from the fear and distrust toward Russians among the various ethnic groups in the former Soviet Empire, the Bolsheviks did too.

In the United States, plutocrats have found politicians who exploit ethnic tensions to convince commoners to vote for the corporate state. Right wing media has revived the "old guard." Americans' reverence for individualism was twisted around to exalt the one percent, who according to the myth got rich because they are "rugged individualists." The elites preserve plutocracy with the help of glib hawkers, hired in legions to remind everyone else that the wealthy have earned every penny of their wealth, and deserve to keep it all. The pitch was not always effective, but perseverant delivery convinced enough voters to swing elections that any attempts to reduce income inequality are manifestations of "socialist plots to destroy America." By the 1960's, the leaders of the Republican Party were true believers in the myth of rugged individualism. Along with this myth went demonizing of the national government. States' Rights were lauded once more, especially in the South. In 1964 Barry Goldwater won five states in the Deep South by renouncing the Republican Party's anti-slavery roots and advocating state sovereignty. Richard Nixon parlayed this "Southern Strategy" into a close election win four years later. In 1980 Ronald Reagan could begin his campaign in Philadelphia, Mississippi (where three civil rights workers had been murdered) by stating "I believe in States' Rights." He went on to win in a landslide over Jimmy Carter, a born-again Christian from Georgia.

With the Republican Party's metamorphosis from the Party of Lincoln to one more comfortable with Jefferson Davis, the plutocrats took power by exploiting hate. Powerful as the emotion is, it happened that many supporters of the plutocrats' victory also belonged to fundamentalist sects, and still do. Therefore, in defiance of the teachings of that Nazarine, God and Mammon had become close friends. With God on our side, we found ourselves poised to wage war—because we believe we are right. With war using up surplus production without materially improving the lot of commoners, the upper classes solidified their rule.

Superficially, the evangelical, rugged individualist, racist plutocracy we now have is the opposite of Oceania under atheistic Ingsoc. But to those who believe God is Power, the end justifies the means. And the means to acquire power are through harnessing an army of true believers. Conversely, true believers are not hampered by the philosophy of their creed, so long as they have a cause they can sacrifice for. And the ideal world of a century ago, in which there were no communists, terrorists or atomic bombs, when everybody was God-fearing and families stuck together no matter what, sounds very pleasant. And if non-whites were subject to rule by whites, that was also a part of that halcyon time. If we must return the robber barons to absolute power over the culture, that, in the eyes of the true believer, is also a small price to pay.

Just as the ideology fueling despotism is unimportant, the details by which despots seize power are not identical. One thing stands out: the leaders publicly believe that they alone possess the cures for mankind's despair. They practice doublethink expertly, and they save the "God is Power" confession until they have us locked into the Ministry of Love. In Orwell's story, the aftermath of atomic war established the three autocratic super-states. While this did not happen in the real world, the core nations: The United States, Russia, and China, nevertheless hold sway over large extra-territorial empires, and are ruled by entrenched robber baron elites. As we learn with increasing, detailed frequency, the elites can watch and hear everything we do and say. The unstinting cruelty of previous regimes, extrapolated by Orwell into its logical conclusion, is avoided for the most part. Rulers have learned that brute force is a last resort, expensive and only temporarily effective, to be used in isolated exemplary cases.

Though they could employ large-scale torture, imprisonment and terror to maintain power, the elites of the world prefer not to, mainly for public relations purposes. With everyone sold on the concept of freedom, police state tactics are generally unpopular, and this reality renders the elites in all areas vulnerable to overthrow. Those who value freedom can take advantage of the fact that we are not in an absolute terror state—yet. If the Thought Police ever start vaporizing our neighbours in the night, we have probably lost our freedom beyond recall.

Power feeds on itself, and everything else. It must expand, and when people consent to giving the elites power over anybody, the elites will never stop until they have power over everybody. Benign dictatorships reserve the right to stop being benign. Liberty cannot preserve itself, nor can it be selfishly hoarded. If we would have it, we must insist that everyone has it, and we must watch our rulers as we ought never allow them to watch us.

28

Individualism and Society

"I said it then, and I say now, that while there is a lower class I am in it, and while there is a criminal element I am of it, and while there is a soul in prison I am not free." - Eugene V. Debs, upon sentencing for sedition, 11/18/1918

"It is well for those who hug the present and want to preserve it as it is not to play with mass movements." - Eric Hoffer, *The True Believer*

Society exists to provide maximum fulfillment in the lives of all individuals. Practical people know this ideal has never been reached and given human nature, will always be beyond attainment.

Still, the reason for society is unchanged. We have reached a stage in history where the individual is highly valued, yet corporate values dominate the lives of us all. The individual left to his own devices has a rough time. Still, even in a world of seven billions, the individual has greater chances for personal fulfillment than at any time since the end of the Neolithic age, due in large part to the material and mechanical advances the race has made since the Renaissance. These advances have occurred through a happy combination of individual efforts and social cooperation. Humanity could make monumental progress from where it now stands, but this depends on how we behave. The need for each of us to exercise his or her full potential while simultaneously functioning within society has never been more urgent.

We must all be aware and watchful, if we are to manage the fearsome challenges we face in the early Third Millennium. Turning our potential into real human progress requires us to understand and accept the fact that Margaret Thatcher was wrong: there is such a thing as society. Those who refuse to act on this fundamental reality effectively surrender the sum of material advancement made by humanity, to the control of the rulers of the corporate state. If we hoard our individuality, we are left, in O'Brien's words, "alone….beyond history." We all know true believers whose exaltations of rugged individualism lead them to support a strong corporate state, simply because the corporate elites, like the libertarians, share their belief in no taxes, no government. Libertarians tolerate exploitation of the state's power by well-placed individuals, yet they view cooperative actions to use the state to help commoners as anti-democratic. Arguing with such true believers is a frustrating waste of time. Our energies will be better spent working with those who share our vision of economic, social and political democracy, or in dialogue with open-minded people.

Libertarians have been hoodwinked by glib advocates for the elites, who revere not the individual, but their own individual ambitions, which come down to domination of everyone else. The supporters of the elites in the class war are better left alone. They prefer it that way. There are numerous organizations dedicated to economic and social justice, to enabling our democracy to function for the benefit of everyone.   These deserve our time and resources. There will be mistakes, letdowns, and abject failures, and the blessings of liberty will probably never be entirely secure. Functioning societies, built by human beings, are the products of hard work, performed cooperatively. Since the development of hunter-gatherer clans, mankind's success has depended on cooperation.

Cooperation, of course, is not coercion. The rugged individualist is an attractive figure in our mythology. But to view the universe realistically, we must see whom this monumental "hero" is standing over. We who honestly value our individualism can only protect it in concert with other individuals who value theirs. Otherwise we will be cut down, one-by-one, by any "hero" who can hire a few underlings to do the cutting. The rest of us will be absorbed, as always, into an obedient underclass composed of a persecuted Middle and an abused, ignorant Low. This scenario is happening now, as it did throughout history...as it did in *1984*.

Our government structure is still sound, as it was when established more than two centuries ago. Though always in need of improvements, it is basically a system of governing which allows all citizens to strive together to assure the greatest potential for individualism to flourish. Over time we have expanded the right of citizenship to more people, which shows that what we have, for the most part, works, when we work it. When citizens participate in government's functioning, the government we have serves most of us well. When we walk away (as we did beginning in the seventies, when the end of the Vietnam War and the resignation of Richard Nixon led many of us to believe the good times were here to stay) those who remain to govern are likely to be self-serving. Considering the tremendous scale of human ambition and creativity, these stragglers will find ways to rig our system—any system—to their own selfish ends. Absolute power has always been their end, and modern times have not changed human nature.

Though the Law of the Land has been hijacked by modern robber barons, it is written to enable the people to peacefully defeat hijackers. So the true conservatives are still "We the People." We will regain our democracy only by working together, making mistakes, compromising, and learning from our mistakes. This worthwhile effort is challenging, sometimes trying, often frustrating. And it is never finished.

29

Smart Revolution

"If one is to rule, and to continue ruling, one must be able to dislocate the sense of reality. For the secret of rulership is to combine a belief in one's own infallibility with the power to learn from past mistakes." - *1984*

O'Brien takes a lot of trouble to build Winston's hopes, then beat him into submission until he loves Big Brother. Most of us are not really that important, though many executives in the corporate world routinely gain the trust of underlings only to turn on them when the time comes. Orwell shows us some of the horrors endured by our fellows in some countries, which we too could be enduring if we allow current trends to go unchallenged. Since *1984* was published in 1949, we have seen these horrors come true to some extent. We have also been able to fight back. America and the Anglophone nations included in Orwell's Oceania, retain their freedoms, at least de jure. At the same time, some people in Orwell's Eurasia and Eastasia, and in many parts of the lands that would be disputed colonies, have achieved some freedom. Overall, the world has at least the structures in place for far greater freedom than Orwell predicted.

Having died on the cusp of the electronic revolution, Orwell could not have predicted the monumental growth of communication or its growing availability to all people at all levels. These technologies have enabled rival governments to work together to achieve mutual goals in ways that were unimaginable at the end of WWII, when the Iron Curtain was lowered. While electronic media have allowed greater freedom to people everywhere, they have also enabled the corporate states and military-industrial complexes to maintain greater control over societies than ever before.

O'Brien's contempt for the fascists and Bolshe-viks reflects the Ingsoc Party's perception that these pioneers in totalitarianism had the right ideas but lacked the sense to take them all the way, to seize and keep total power, as Big Brother had done. As the Ingsoc Party learned, so have the world's ruling classes learned from the mistakes of the vanquished Nazis and the now vanished Bolsheviks. Modern rulers have learned they can control people more effectively without the insanity and huge expense of mass purges, vicious mental and physical tortures, and sprawling prison systems. These tools are used sparingly now, much to everyone's satisfaction. Still, worldwide the resources are here for going back to old- fashioned ways.

At the dawn of the Third Millennium, populations are controlled subtly, with economic insecurity and a constant barrage of selective information, usually called advertising, as the main tools. Unlike members of the Inner Party, modern elites still love material possessions. Flamboyant displays of wealth seem to cow the lower classes into submission. Whether materialism will lead to the elites' downfall is for the future to decide, but elites are for the nonce entrenched. It appears that masses can be easily controlled if they are convinced they are free. "Freedom is Slavery." Similarly, people will tolerate a great deal of income inequality if they believe some day they could be rich. This popular myth has allowed the elites to snatch virtually all the planet's economic growth over the past forty years.

Supporting the myth that anybody could get rich is the cruel conviction that the poor are to blame for their poverty. When people are steeped in this belief there is no reason for slaves to complain to each other about their plight. By convincing the masses that they deserve their privations, the elites have acquired wealth and power on a scale unseen in a century. They have bankrupted the economy with wars and ruined the middle class, without having to resort to police state excesses.

Many people know that wealth and power are increasingly consolidated with the one percent, and many are offering organized opposition to this trend. Yet knowledge and resistance are in most important issues ineffective. The wealthy control the economy, growing richer while the people's political representatives are unwilling or unable to do anything to help the disadvantaged —although most people want to redistribute at least some of the wealth. The Uppers in our society have withstood challenges from Socialists, Populists, Progressives, Wobblies, Unions, hippies and peace movements. They have studied how to prevent the rise of serious movements that oppose their supremacy. The Occupy demonstrations and the election of 2012 did prevent a thorough takeover by the servants of the elites, but the power of the corporate state remains.

With the growth of wealth and power at the top of the economic ladder, the elites seem to be in an impregnable position. They can endure and outlast any opposition, while economic reality forces those below to retreat. The message we are sent is clear: resistance is futile. The message is every bit as arrogant as O'Brien's gloating over Winston's starved, broken, imprisoned body. Rationality tells us that since the Uppers started the class war, we commoners had better surrender. Still, some of us remain "insane", being unwilling to give up yet. We are challenged to find more effective means of resistance, of making the changes that most of us want. We are still at liberty to seek out alternative information to the massive propaganda tsunami. We owe it to our economic condition, as well as our peace of mind and our liberty, to do so.

Censorship has not been necessary because the corporate rulers control information with sheer overwhelming volume. They have total confidence in their propaganda machine to bury any concepts of the truth that might actually threaten their hegemony. But since the truth is as yet available, we are obligated to seek, find and share the truth. What others do with it is beyond our control, but we must personally act on it, and work with others who believe as we do. Since we know that something is wrong, that the current economic and power structure is unjust, we are channeling Winston Smith. We are the ones the elites fear. We are the ones they will seek to isolate, to defeat one by one. They will try to convince us to give up on ourselves.

30

Together

"Do you understand that you are alone? You are outside history, you are non-existent." - *1984*

"Some of the biggest men in the United States, in the field of commerce and manufacture, are afraid of somebody, are afraid of something. They know that there is a power somewhere so organized, so subtle, so watchful, so interlocked, so complete, so pervasive, that they had better not speak above their breath when they speak in condemnation of it." - Woodrow Wilson, *The New Freedom, 1912*

Again, I must restate the belief that perhaps the most stubborn obstacle to human progress in modern times is the fact that Joseph Stalin and Mao Zedong styled themselves "socialists." The reigns of terror they ordered have given our corporate elites a priceless advantage in any discussion of economic policy. Thanks to the Gulags in Russia and Great Leaps Forward in Red China, it is fairly easy to overlook the horrors the lords of capital have inflicted. Yet as Woodrow Wilson told us before the Bolshevik Revolution began, fascism was already gaining sway over the "Land of the Free." Campaigning Wilson warned us of the threat of corporate rule. Then President Wilson imprisoned Eugene Debs for sedition, which reveals how frighteningly powerful the corporate state already was. And as we know, its power has not decreased in the following century. All presidents must serve the corporate state and the military-industrial complex, whether or not the people elect them for that purpose. And the corporate state's power hides behind that pretty myth of "rugged individualism." Any attempts or proposals to use government to make life better for the majority can be effortlessly attacked as a socialistic threat to our sacred individual freedoms.

Though the Constitution establishes a system for effective government by the people, it cannot guarantee freedom and justice for all unless Americans continually watch their government. Many Americans harbour deep revulsion toward the concept of government, going back to revolutionary times, when government meant divine-right monarchy. Then it was physically possible to move beyond the frontier line and survive or perish by toughness, luck and wits. But people kept moving west, and eventually the Pacific Ocean stood in the way of further escape from the evils of civilization. Still, a pervasive mindset exists among Americans that all individuals are only free when they can completely eliminate government. This ideology, added to memories of communist terror, creates powerful distrust of any trappings of social polity. Robber barons, who also despise governmental interference, adeptly exploit the pioneering, rugged individualistic sensibilities. The result is that many people who despise tyranny elect politicians who support corporate control of government…which is fascism.

The volume of doublethink necessary to enable people to support wars and their by-products: state surveillance and stifling of dissent, mistrust of certain ethnic groups and religions, racial prejudice, official lying and suppression of voting rights (among others) and still revere rugged individualism is astounding. Convincing these believers otherwise is probably impossible. We who respectfully disagree, who believe that there is such a thing as society, that government serves a purpose, that the elimination of legitimate government creates a power vacuum that despots are ready to fill, must realize that libertarian true believers are more interested in arguing than polite dialogue about solving society's problems. We waste time and energy (direly needed commodities) in the fruitless exercise of playing their game. We who know that governing is imperfect, ongoing work, had probably better get to work. The job ahead is massive.

We need to work together to reclaim our democratic government for ourselves. We need to work with organizations that honestly represent our interests, and we need to support politicians who profess a desire to address our concerns, and at the same time we need to lean on them to insist that they do. All politicians need money, and we need to root out the means by which corporations and wealthy individuals buy politicians. We need to put a stop to such methods as we find them, ever mindful that clever crooks are always looking for new ways to rig the game. The winnings and losses in this game are serious: how we distribute what we produce; whether we have war or peace; who goes to jail; who prospers, who will endure privation; what we may say and do; who pays attention. Those who simply dismiss government, like those who want to make up the rules as they go along, are like everyone else entitled to their opinions. But they do not get to wreck what the adults are trying to build.

The myth of the successful rugged individualist taps into the conviction that everyone needs to earn his living. It is understood that all who can, should work. But since the beginning of the industrial age, machines have done more and more of the physical, and recently much of the mental work that people had done, since humans began to plant crops. Furthermore, market economies have never been able to foresee and prevent boom-and-bust cycles, which leave many productive working people idle and impoverished. Are these situations the result of natural forces, or are they manmade? If they are manmade, does it not stand to reason that people can and should do something about them? How we honestly answer these questions will define what we do.

Aside from doing nothing, to let people suffer, freeze, lose all they have, and go hungry until the magical marketplace again creates enough paying work for everyone, there are two other options, both of which have been tried from time-to-time. One is to reduce the workload, allowing more people to share in the work that needs to be done. Reductions of this type have resulted in the standard forty-hour workweek. Another option is to employ people in public works, to do things that need doing but cannot be efficiently done for a profit. Paying people to maintain the basic structures that allow the rest of us to engage in the profitable commerce that provides jobs is a practice going back to the end of the Neolithic age. Society, like every household, needs maintaining and rebuilding. The maintenance of society of course depends on competent management. But to dismiss all government as bad means essentially doing nothing.

Shortened workweeks, improved working conditions, and public works projects are not the initiatives of any ruling class. Social changes to make life better for the commoners can only come from the non-elites. Unions, pressure groups, and public service organizations are the means by which the common people improve their common lot. Yet, the upper classes also benefit from a stable, prosperous, healthy, working society. The question arises: are the Highs, in opposing better living for the two lower groups, rational? The answer, it would seem, is obvious. This brings us back to the notion that economic inequality results in social superiority —the ability to order others about. And we can conclude that at least some elites know this and like it, and fully subscribe to the notion that "God is Power." When most commoners are economically comfortable, they are not likely to defer to their prosperous countrymen, so merely having great wealth loses much of its charm. It is, after all, only money.

Libertarians, like everyone else (including the very rich) take advantage of social services, infrastructure, and government protection. Yet libertarians claim total self-reliance. There is probably no use arguing with them. Time and energy can be more profitably employed working with others toward common goals. "A more perfect union" means comprehensive social polity, a society in which all are respected and granted opportunities to prosper and fulfill themselves as individuals—all guaranteed and protected by an elected government, supervised by active citizens. Collective action is essential. Citizens who work together for the common good tend to know and trust one another, and are better able to resist the manipulations of the corporate state, than are isolated individuals who do nothing more than guard their domiciles.

It comes as no surprise that the elites despise government. Effective government would not allow them to obtain enormous wealth when others must go without basic needs. But government, to be effective, to assure "liberty and justice for all," depends on large-scale citizen participation. It should come as no surprise that the elites constantly remind us that resistance is futile. No man on a white horse—no Uncle, Chairman, Duce, Fuhrer, or Big Brother—will ever get absolute power and still rule benignly. Eternal vigilance, the price of liberty, translates into eternal action.

The good news is that most people who promote the best in human nature are pleasant company.

31

Life Goes On

"It does not take a majority to prevail. But rather an irate, tireless minority, keen on setting the brushfires of freedom in the minds of men." - Samuel Adams

"We have to have fun while trying to stave off the forces of darkness because we hardly ever win, so it's the only fun we get to have." - Molly Ivins, *The Nation Magazine*, 11/17/2003

Popular culture took on a witty irreverence from the mid-sixties to the mid-seventies, a decade which saw tremendous social changes worldwide. In America the irreverence was enough to topple traditions and power structures. Unfortunately, it turned out that after the Civil Rights advances, the Watergate trials, and the end of war in Vietnam, we still had problems, and Americans turned serious by the early eighties. Ronald Reagan's well-known one-liners were part of his act, not heartfelt mirth. Reagan's strength came from his ability to convince people that he related to them, that he shared their dour vengefulness, and that those who disagreed with him, and them, could be dismissed with a joke. America had a job to do, a job which had been slowed down by a decade of parties and protests. We could get things done only by going back to the way things were before all that nonsense started.

Communism was the deadly foreign enemy, to be dealt with not by cowardly détente, but bold defiance. The Reds were helped within America by the drug culture, the lazy poor, overindulged youngsters, and whiners who simply hated America. We had wasted too much time trying to accommodate them. America was in trouble because Americans had had been too nice. But that was over. A successful actor of questionable talent, Reagan honed his major role as America's peerless leader over three decades. He played the presidential role well. He was more than a president: old but spry, wise without being smart, decisive without being overly thoughtful, kind but strict, angry without losing his cool. He remembered the good days, and knew how to lead us back to them. He played the part of "Big Grandpa" and it would seem Americans ardently desired such a person's leadership. At any rate, he won the California governorship twice, and the presidency twice, in landslides every time.

His opposition, though numerous, was ineffective. Reagan was against drugs, crime, welfare, and godless communism. Who could rationally be for those things? He was for self-reliance, rugged individualism, law-and-order, and national strength. Who could be against those? From the Vietnam fiasco, the civil rights disruptions, Watergate, the energy crisis, the economic downturn, the Iranian hostage crisis, the Soviet takeover of Afghanistan, to name a few, it was obvious that America had problems. Only stern measures could get the country back on top again, where it belonged. The party and the free ride were over. The country needed to grow up.

Who better to show us the way, than a grandfatherly figure? If Father knew best (as he did in the fifties) how wise must Grandpa be?

Down went taxes and government spending, though not at the huge levels the right-wing spokespeople were bragging about. Up went defense, and America fought several tiny but popular wars (the most famous being our "triumph" over Grenada) at the same time daring our Soviet enemies to try us in a nuclear war. And while Americans were enthusiastic at first about these initiatives, the fact was that Americans overwhelmingly approved of government services and knew they would have to pay for them. Nuclear war was never a popular idea, once people thought about it. The rightwing needed a true cause, which it got by co-opting fundamentalist Christianity into its force. Reagan openly cultivated the evangelicals, and they joined a political dialogue they had previously avoided, supporting Reagan, a half-hearted churchgoer, overwhelmingly. Jimmy Carter, a practicing evangelical Christian, got scant approval from his fellows.

With God on our side, there was nothing America could not do. A strict God would guide us to basic righteous order in the universe. A strict God demanded the country's leadership to be strict. Unions were broken, workers told to be grateful for their jobs. A nation that had been looking at lessening the penalties for drugs began to seriously consider testing everyone's urine. Attempts to reduce crime by rehabilitation were replaced by harsh punishment. Anti-poverty programs were replaced by a single admonishment: get a job. Behind the orders from an almighty creator, the business establishment could regain its status of omnipotence. Where business and government managers had been experimenting with teamwork, seeking input from workers, the management style reverted to giving orders and expecting instant obedience. It was time to toughen up. A wise grandpa, guided by an all-knowing deity, would show us how.

The only flaw in Reagan's plan was that it implemented social and economic policies that had previously led to the Great Depression. Those who dared to say so were conveniently ignored. The rich grew immensely richer while everyone else stayed about the same or grew poorer, despite rising worker productivity. By 2008 Americans could see how deep a hole they had dug for themselves. Economic disaster struck nearly everyone who was not wealthy. The middle class and working poor were stuffed into a single crowded class, universally without hope of upward mobility. The major financial monopolies were tumbling into bankruptcy, and since they controlled the country, they got the despised government to rescue them. When Barack Obama tried to do the same for the newly unemployed, newly impoverished, the elites had their minions threaten shut down of government, threats which many voters applauded. The party that serves the one percent exclusively did lose enough elections to put it in a defensive position, yet its members refuse to cooperate even slightly with the party that serves the one percent while trying to help everyone else just a little. At a time that screams for economic and social action, almost nothing is getting done.

Tea Party Patriots, clinging to a blind reverence for self-reliance, are financed and exploited by the one percent. In the past the Tea Partiers were called "Know Nothings" or the "Lunatic Fringe". They nurture a vitriolic hate for government, though they benefit as much as everyone else from the social safety net. Though a minority, they are irate and tireless, and firmly believe they are setting "brushfires of freedom", which the one percent exploits endlessly. Though most of their beliefs will not translate well onto the real world, their ability to win struggles should not be underestimated.

Liberals and progressives, people who want government of by and for the people to work, are not of the true believer mindset. We are today's actual conservatives, desiring to preserve and improve a status quo that we honestly believe is basically sound. We are practical people who do not fit in with mass movements on the left or right. Our desires to find common ground with the Tea Partiers put us at a disadvantage. The Tea Partiers, like all fanatics, are uninterested in dialogue. They want their way, and when they get it, they are still dissatisfied. "We lay waste our powers," trying to debate them. Doing so we unwittingly serve the cause of the corporate elites.

We are the Winston Smiths of post-*1984* Oceania. We know something is amiss, that all is not well in the sanitized picture of the world we see. We have advantages that Winston lacked. Hidden behind the incessant propaganda barrage paid for by the corporate elites, the truth is available, to those who seek it. If we know we are being lied to, have we any recourse other than to act on it? Will the reality go away? Will we ultimately learn to love Big Brother? If not, then we must change a power structure of terrible strength. Big Brother may be watching us, but we can still tell him to mind his own business. While we still have these assets, we are obliged to act—together. If we ever reach a point where we must cling to a tiny news clipping before tossing it down the memory hole, it will be too late.

The military-industrial complex is geared to win any war, so non-violence is essential. We must recognize that members of the NRA wing of the Tea Party would rather put down a violent revolution of socialists, minorities, and poor people, than to actually take on a heavily armed police state. Our own Revolution being one of the rare exceptions, violent revolutions merely change despots. Our founders set up mechanisms for us to bring about change without resorting to violence. Those mechanisms are still available. We will need to use them to their fullest. The elites, learning from their mistakes, have hijacked our constitutional government. Learning from our mistakes, we the people can take them back. The process, even if non-violent, is arduous.

Being human, we can make our fun. Being human, we are entitled to it. Anyone who has observed a protest demonstration will notice that the ones who are protesting corporate rule, the next war, or state-sponsored injustice, are much happier than the Tea Partiers who attend in the hopes of interrupting, in the service of the corporate state. This is true even though we are usually on the losing side. In addition to common decency, we have the ability to laugh, which is a potent weapon. Not only does an honest sense of humour make the toil more bearable, the other side has no defense against it. Molly Ivins was right: bullies win most fights, so we had better learn to enjoy the struggle.

If we can have fun, we stand a better than even chance.

We are in good company, and for the most part we enjoy one another. We have before us an enormous task, but for whatever reason we have taken it on. Like Winston Smith, deciding to write his diary, we know our actions are crazy. If we make it fun, we could succeed together.

We are the majority.

Glossary

SOME TERMS FROM ORWELL'S 1984

1) **<u>Airstrip One</u>** -   The INGSOC designation for the British Isles. Beginning in WWII, the U.S. Air Force had used the islands to bomb Axis targets in Europe.

2) **<u>Big Brother</u>** - The Leader of the English Socialist (INGSOC) Party, therefore of all Oceania.   Though revered, even deified, in party propaganda, he is never actually seen. So intense is the propaganda that no one truly remembers what his real name was, or if in fact he ever was an actual person. It is understood that he will never die. Similar to "Uncle Joe" Stalin.

3) **<u>Doublethink</u>** -   The mental exercise of holding two opposing thoughts in the mind at

the same time, believing both to be absolutely true.   Doublethink is practiced constantly in Party circles, allowing members to accept whatever the current Party Line might be, even if it contradicts the Line presented only a short time before.

4) **INGSOC** - English Socialism, the program of the political party ruling Oceania. Similar to National Socialism = Nazism.

5) **Inner Party** - A small cadre of leaders of the Party. Oceania's upper class.

6) **Ministry of Love** - The agency wherein the Thought Police tortures those accused/convicted of Thoughtcrime until they lose all self-identity and finally love Big Brother.

7) **Ministry of Truth** - The agency responsible for creating and distributing propaganda to the residents of Oceania. Winston Smith works here.

8) **O'Brien** - The antagonist in 1984. He befriends, then betrays Winston Smith, and finally supervises Winston's rehabilitation by torture.

9) **Oceania** - The totalitarian super-state where Winston Smith lives. It consists of North

and South America, Australia, New Zealand, South Africa, and the British Isles, or Airstrip One.

10) **<u>Outer Party</u>** - The subservient group of the INGSOC party. Oceania's middle class. Winston and Julia are members.

11) **<u>The Party</u>** - The English Socialist (INGSOC) Party, the only legal political party in Oceania.

12) **<u>Proles</u>** - Members of the "working class", the Proletariat. All citizens who do not belong to The Party.

13) **<u>Room 101</u>** - The place within the Ministry of Love containing "the worst thing in the world." This of course varies depending on the individual political prisoner. All prisoners ultimately go here, to be tortured to the point where they will betray anyone and everyone, and mean that betrayal to the core of their souls, in order to gain reprieve from "the worst thing in the world." All prisoners give up the final semblance of their selves here.

14) **<u>Telescreens</u>** - Two-way televisions, watched by all individuals, and used by the Thought Police to watch all individuals. There is

one in every apartment, and it cannot be turned off.

15) **<u>Thoughtcrime</u>** - The only serious crime that a citizen of Oceania can commit. Thinking that The Party could be wrong about anything, ever, constitutes this capital offense. More traditional crimes such as robbery, assault, or murder, are treated as mere misdemeanors. The true crime, it turns out, is "thought."

16) **<u>Thought Police</u>** - Oceania's secret police.

17) **<u>Two-minute Hates</u>** - Activities of the citizens in which all are required to participate in expressing their hatred for the current enemies of the regime. These exercises typically last two minutes.

18) **<u>Vaporization</u>** - The fate of anyone arrested by the Thought Police. Usually it involves being dragged from bed at night and taken to the Ministry of Love. When this happens, the vaporized one becomes an unperson, and all are expected to forget he ever existed.

About the Author

A baby-boomer and lifelong Californian, I have always had an aversion to excessive authority. Currently I am dedicated to endowing our children with a cleaner, freer, saner, more provident Earth than the one we appear to be leaving them. At the same time I have acquired enough honest humility to know that as far as tangible results are concerned, there is very little I can do. People of the future will make the best of the world they are born into. They will muddle along, and hopefully survive (as we have) despite what was done by those who came before. Still, to my mind, this realistic viewpoint does not excuse me from doing the best I can while I am here, to improve things for those who will be here a while longer.

So I have written this book.

I was educated in public schools and public colleges. I earned a living in civil service. I am a family man and an involved citizen. My experience has been devoid of the sort of adventures we like to read about or see in the movies. Yet I have learned that any life, consciously lived, is by nature adventurous. As my personal adventure nears the finis, I am far less prone to fear for life, liberty, or property than I was in the past. Though far from wealthy, I am comfortable. I find myself now in a situation where I am more immune to exterior threats to "straighten up and fly right" than I ever was, or will be again.

Like so many others of my age and circumstances, I am seeking challenges to my physical, mental, and emotional limitations. Rather than find mountains to climb, oceans to swim, deserts to cross, or jungles to explore, I want to raise the risks, to challenge the grossest fear I know: that means speaking truth to power.

My quest to challenge the power structure did not start with this book, nor will it end here. But this book is a big part of that quest.

Gregg Ward Matson, Elk Grove, CA, 2014

CPSIA information can be obtained at www.ICGtesting.com
Printed in the USA
BVOW04s1350020414

349509BV00001B/57/P